Tempus ORAL HISTORY *Series*

voices of
Kent's Hop Gardens

Wartime evacuees who volunteered to go hopping at Chambers Farm, near Maidstone.

Cover illustration: VE Day was celebrated at Whitbreads, like everywhere else, in May 1945 (courtesy of the Hop Farm Country Park).

Tempus ORAL HISTORY *Series*

voices of
Kent's Hop Gardens

Compiled by
Hilary Heffernan

TEMPUS

First published 2000
Copyright © Hilary Heffernan, 2000

Tempus Publishing Limited
The Mill, Brimscombe Port,
Stroud, Gloucestershire, GL5 2QG

ISBN 0 7524 2090 9

Typesetting and origination by
Tempus Publishing Limited
Printed in Great Britain by
Midway Clark Printing, Wiltshire

A children's tea party at the Hop Festival, on the Whitbread Hop Farm in the 1940s.

Contents

Acknowledgements

This book is dedicated to the many hop-pickers who have contacted me with their wonderful reminiscences. We recall with affection the days when folk knew how to make the best of life with what little they had and to entertain themselves without the need to rely on television or computer games. From the tales I am told I know how much those days are missed and how a way of life expected to go on forever came to a grinding halt when Progress took over. I am convinced that somewhere in Heaven there must be a secluded hop garden for hoppers who leave this Earth. Here they may go to pick choice cones of Goldings or Fuggles to their hearts' content, singing with the angels around camp fires in the evenings and enjoying a pint of the best seated on barrel benches outside 'The Cloud on High' free house. My sincere thanks to contributors who contacted me with their reminiscences and photographs included in this book. Contributions have been individually credited after each reminiscence. I apologize to any person or persons whose picture I have used and whose acknowledgement may have been inadvertently omitted. If, when you have read this book, you think, 'I have a hopping story to tell that should be remembered and shared,' I will be delighted to hear from you. Please remember that these are reminiscences; they are memories as people recall them from as long as sixty or seventy years ago. We all embellish incidents in our minds, even if only slightly, so if the geography of a farm is not described the way you remember it, the name is spelt otherwise or an incident is related slightly differently to the way you knew it, remember these are not events set in stone, but personal recollections recounted the way the teller enjoys telling them.

HH

Oast houses at Whitbreads farm, Beltring, in 1989.

Introduction

The earliest record of the use of hops was in 597 BC when Jews in Babylon used them for flavouring a home-made brew while in captivity. In Britain, Kentish hop-growing was once a thriving industry employing thousands of workers. Since wholesale mechanization in the early 1960s, employment has dwindled to a few hundred people working the gardens. In its heyday between 1860 and 1880 over 70,000 acres of prime Kent land were given over to hop cultivation. In this year, 2000, less than 10,000 acres are in use for this important crop and it is still declining.

Happy choruses of 'If you go down hopping, Hopping down in Kent…' resoundingly sung by field workers nimbly picking their way along the drifts are now replaced by the mechanical clatter of machines stripping bines of their harvests. In the thirties and fifties whole streets of hoppers came down from London in droves, leaving their door keys dangling just inside their letter boxes on bits of string ready for when they got home weeks later. They caught the early morning Hoppers' Special train from London Bridge, before spreading across Kent to various farms. This was their one holiday of the year for which they had waited since the last day of the previous season, while looking forward to joyful reunions with old friends. For three to seven weeks, according to the size of their farmer's 'garden', they joined home-dwellers from local villages to gather in the rich harvest across the county, working an eight or nine-hour day, five and a half to six days a week, to earn a few pounds by the end of the season.

Some gardens hired local workers exclusively, but in September large hop farms required a small army of pickers to complete harvesting in the short time available before hop cones started spoiling on the bine, so picking was largely undertaken by outsiders: Londoners, folk who followed seasonal work across from other counties and travelling gypsies, including fruit and potato pickers, came down in their droves. Occasionally hopping was used as a health cure when a doctor, anxious about the fitness of his impoverished patients and keen to get them out of the heavily polluted London air, ordered them to go hop-picking for the season. This was at a time when it was quite common for Londoners to die from the choking effects of smog – a lethal combination of smoke and fog which eventually prompted the introduction of the Clean Air Act. The difference between town and country air was more marked than now: air in towns and cities was laden with carbon monoxide and particles from industrial and domestic fumes, while country air was fresh and clean.

Most city pickers went to the same farm year after year. Regular hoppers traditionally kept their own hut on the farm, sometimes handed on from grandparents or parents. Farmers were mostly content to allow workers to leave bits and sticks of furniture in their hut from year to year and to regularly employ the same families.

Although hoppers guarded their privileges fiercely there were certain aspects of being in the country that tempted some to break the rules, such as scrumping fruit or vegetables from nearby orchards and fields, appropriating the occasional egg or 'lost' chicken or helping themselves to a sweet too near the edge of the counter to resist. Consequences for such daring could be dire. An indulgent farmer, knowing the family, may turn a blind eye or give a stern warning, but if

Mrs Laura Rule and family.

thievery was blatant, stricter farmers would have the family packed up and off their land, never to return. There were occasional drunken fights but these were settled with minimum fuss and the police were only called in on rare occasions.

The Salvation Army held a high profile in the hop fields and their monthly magazine, *The Deliverer*, ran regular features about hoppers, sometimes with a high moral tone but also with tolerance for an aggregation of people that, in the early years, were so poor they were glad to have one decent meal a day and to get away from the city grind and grime for just a few short weeks each year. The Salvation Army did a marvellous job in the fields, not only saving souls but at times also saving lives. They tended injuries, provided tea and comfort, lent a shoulder to cry on and helped out with the necessities of life where possible. Hoppers enjoyed the Sunday morning services, singing the old hymns such as 'Onward Christian Soldiers', 'There is a Green Hill Far Away' or 'All things Bright and Beautiful', standing out on the village green with the Sally Army's brass band playing with gusto in the background. In many cases the Army came from Citadels in the same areas as the hoppers and already knew the families and their problems and background which helped when assessing where the greatest needs were. The Salvationists showed a great deal of tolerance and indulgence towards the hop-pickers and their foibles, although at times they seemed to have considered them a race apart. In Victorian times the Sally Army was particularly down on heavy drinking, rightly seeing this as a waste of a family's precious income which could have been spent on essential food or clothing. Kevin Parry has a collection of nineteenth-century Salvation Army magazines from which are contributed the several extracts included here.

When the season was in full swing, an uneasy alliance was made between city and country folk. Many villagers, particularly pub and shop owners, saw the London hoppers as invaders, bringing fleas, thieving ways and rowdy behaviour to their quiet villages. Pubs charged a deposit on glasses etc. when serving pints to hoppers who would otherwise help any useful items of crockery and glassware to find its way back to their hop huts. Small boys earned extra pocket money by returning glasses retrieved from under the plank seats outside the pub, sometimes without the drinker's knowledge. Bottles were at a premium and it was profitable to pick up any empties and return these for cash. I remember that Tizer bottles fetched a penny a time, which was good money in those days. Pickers recalled seeing wire netting nailed over the open counters and across shop windows to obstruct any Londoners who may have an eye to pilfering. Some owners locked a half door in place so hoppers had to call over it to the shopkeeper before they could buy their necessities. Ration books were still in force until the 1950s, but country shop-keepers tended to be generous with their allocations as food was more readily available in the country, so hoppers were able to eat better than at home. While some farmers forbade hoppers to enter their orchards, others looked kindly on the hungry Londoners and supplied them with windfalls, taking trailer-loads of fruit by tractor to the hop huts and tipping them out on the ground for everyone to help themselves. Jean Pilbeam recalled that 'when hopping was nearly finished the farmer asked if we wanted to go apple picking, so we had another week. That year we went back to London as brown as berries and all the kids wanted to play with us because our hopping box was half-filled with apples.' But despite these small differences between town and country folk, the Londoners eagerly looked forward to their trek into the country. Only a few resented the distrustful attitude of some of the country dwellers, most recognizing there were good reasons for their suspicions. As Alice Heskitt said, she had the London pickers to board at her cottage, saving them from having to sleep in crowded hop huts and cook out in the rain. The hoppers in turn were pleased to return the favour and have her and her husband to stay with them at other times in the year for a city holiday.

Back in London, teachers had no choice but to put up with their errant pupils' absences and it is believed that school holidays were extended to their present six weeks in length to allow for the general exodus for the hop- and fruit-picking seasons: a case of 'if you can't beat 'em, join 'em'. Bright children easily caught up on lessons they missed, but some found it difficult to get over those lost weeks, especially as certain pupils left elementary school at eleven without any intention of going on to an optional secondary education: poor families needed as many breadwinners in the house as possible. Nevertheless, the standard of teaching at council or elementary schools (now state schools) was high and it was less common then for children to leave still unable to read unless their schooling had been stopped at an early age. Bob Orris remembers his school days well and his reminiscence is recorded in chapter two.

At the end of the nineteenth and beginning of the twentieth centuries, non-earners were dead weights in a family, still requiring food and clothing; therefore the pressure was on from early childhood for everyone to pull their weight. Wages were low, barely covering the cost of rent and food, but workers had to accept what they could get. There were strikes and protests for higher pay, but it was risky standing up for your rights in the days before unions gained power and, while many bosses were fair to their workers, at least as many again were prepared to exploit them. The same problem occurred for hop-pickers, as growers were sometimes out-priced in the market by the importation of foreign hops, so farmers hoped to get away with offering the lowest pay possible to workers. This sometimes caused strikes when pickers saw their already meagre wages drop to an unfair level. Pickers were paid by piecework so there was already a problem when the hops were small in a season as they had to work twice as hard to fill a bushel basket as if the hops were large.

Some farmers dismissed aggressive strikers on the spot and this was a large-scale disaster for the families concerned. If word got about that a man or woman were agitators the whole family lost their place at their particular hop farm but were also banned from other farms. This meant that not only could they not earn any extra cash for that season, but also that there was no annual holiday for the family that year, who also lost their hop hut and the opportunity to go hopping with their friends. This alone was a strong deterrent to most would-be strikers.

There was no law against child-worker exploitation and London's poor started work at a very early age, often supplementing the family income from as young as six by running errands for neighbours, breaking up wooden boxes and selling them off as fire kindling or taking on part-time jobs such as butchers' or errand boys, albeit for a pittance. This meant that, while they were not necessarily fully literate, they became adept at maths at an early age, well able to work out what they were worth for any job on offer. Even the worst-educated barrow boy could tell you what 10lb of potatoes cost at a tanner (sixpence) per pound without having to think about it twice or refer to a calculator (the answer is five bob, or five shillings, in case you're wondering!). Money was harder to work out in predecimal currency. There were four farthings to a penny or two ha'pennies (halfpennies); it took twelve pennies to make a shilling (or a 'bob') and twenty shillings to make £1. A guinea was £1 1s. Thoroughbred horses are still sold in guineas. To put this in perspective, imagine receiving a wage slip that read you had earned £3 1s 6½d that week – the rough equivalent of £3.07 today. Your rent was about 5s and the grocery bill for the whole family was about £2 10s (or 50s). That left you with 6s 6½d (approximately 38p today) for your family's clothing, entertainment or emergencies… oh, except that the Man from the Pru (insurance) came every Friday and you'd have to give him 6d for insurance for the family. That left 6s ½d for Dad's fags and beer. There isn't much we could do on 30p today! If the whole family worked hard picking hops, they could earn as much as £40 for their season's work. Compared to a man's weekly wage this was an enormous amount, and shows how important the opportunity to go hopping was for most poor people.

While children mainly saw hopping as a great adventure, they were also expected to pick for at least some of the time. Their efforts in the hop gardens were part of the household contribution towards the family's final pay at the end of the hopping season and even quite small children were expected to do their share of pulling hops off the bine, at least for the morning sessions. Any children too small to reach the wood and canvas hopping bins were given a turned-up open umbrella, bucket or washing up bowl and picked into that. Parents who felt they could afford to reward their offspring's efforts treated them to an ice cream or sweet from one of the many enterprising tradesmen or pedlars who sought trade from the pickers. John Meinke remembers their family shopped 'at various vans that called on the field during the day. Grocers and a butcher came, and bakers with huge lumps of bread pudding.'

Mrs Q. Moody and family outside their hop hut.

After lunch the smaller children either slept by the bins or were allowed off to play, which usually meant exploring the surrounding countryside. By making them work on the hops in the morning, parents gave children a sound awareness of the value of money as well as a sense of the fairness of contributing to the benefit of the whole family rather than letting them think money was readily available. A child was lucky to receive pocket money but it was usually little more than a penny a week and there was no more available once that was spent. Despite the comparatively poor pay and sheer hard work, most ex-hoppers remember those days with great nostalgia and long for the opportunity to have it all again. Going hopping was a form of escapism from the city grind and their only chance to get a change of scenery.

However, there is far more to the hop industry than just the picking and this book encompasses other aspects of the hop, following the development of the bine through to its use in the brewery and into the ever waiting glass.

Hops are a sub-narcotic. Hop pillows, a natural and ancient form of sleep aid, are still available from many herbal shops and some country gardens. 'The youngest in our family is Pat; she was born in 1939, three weeks after war broke out,' says Jean Pilbeam. 'Our mum sometimes put her up at one end of the hop bin and the smell of hops soon sent her to sleep.' A handful of hops kept in a jar is useful for ear-ache: warm the hops gently and apply to the base of the ear. Hops also help to stimulate jaded appetites: young hop shoots can be simmered gently and eaten as a vegetable which tastes something like asparagus.

The Army and Navy Stores advertised compressed hops in the grocery section of their 1933/34 catalogue for 10d a bag and hop leaf mould was available as 'a reliable substitute for stable manure' at 3s per small bag suitable for dressing 25 square yards of land. The advantage of using hop leaf mould over the more usual manure was the milder smell. Whereas the use of stable manure in a garden meant it would produce strong smells for up to a week, especially in hot weather, hop leaf mould has a very mild and far more pleasant aroma.

It is believed that hop plants were first introduced to this country from the continent in medieval times, probably Germany (although some say the Romans brought them when they first came to England). Although first established outside Canterbury in Kent, cultivation eventually spread across to other parts of the country including Worcestershire, Herefordshire, Hampshire and Sussex. Before the Reformation, hops were commonly cultivated in monastery gardens where they were highly regarded for their medicinal properties. Despite the loss of hop farm and garden acreage over the past forty years, Kent is still the county producing the most hops. Mark Dobner, Senior Brewer at Shepherd Neame, explains that a new hop, First Gold, is popular with growers as this strain reaches a maximum height of 10ft and can be grown in a hedgerow system readily available to a picking machine which then picks both sides of an aisle together.

Hop cultivation is a round-the-year job mainly carried out by home-dwellers: workers from surrounding villages or living on the farms, available to work all year and on hand to carry out seasonal jobs required to bring the cones to fruition. Margaret Loader of Bromley remembers her dad was a Londoner who became so adept at various jobs on his regular hop farm that the owner repeatedly asked him to take a permanent job there.

Hop growers each had their own particular preference for when particular jobs were carried out, which meant cultivation methods tended to vary slightly from farm to farm: so while re-stringing may have been done on one farm early in the year, this may not have been carried out until March on the farm next door. Farmers tended to favour one kind of stringing over other methods and some of these are explained in my previous book, *Voices of Kent Hop Pickers*.

All industries tend to have their own vocabulary founded upon the work, tools and processes involved. The hop industry developed its own tools to deal with various aspects of the labour. Where else would you hear of scuppets and hop dogs, oasts and nidgets, firkins and wort coolers or mash tuns?

The opportunities for annual hopping may be gone, but the romance and nostalgia linger on. Wherever two or more hoppers gather together, there will be tales to be told. Some of them are recorded here for you to share, and if you still want to go 'hopping down in Kent' as the old song has it, see the final pages of this book.

CHAPTER 1

The End and the Beginning

Mrs P. Frost's family rest from the picking.

By the end of September, hop picking was over and the army of hoppers unwillingly returned to their London homes. Kent gardens lay bereft of their harvest and over the rest of the year regular workers prepared the fields for next season's crop. Old bines were gathered in but the plants themselves were not cut back until after the nutrients were given time to return to their roots. This sustained them through the winter. Some farmers wound the cut bines into coils, says Ted Bingham, strewing them round areas where animals regularly gathered such as drinking troughs, to act as a kind of drainage so that cattle and sheep were less likely to suffer foot rot through standing in deep mud. Ted worked for Major Bury of Brinley's Farm which at that time employed fifty women to pick. Now, it takes only one worker to do the same job by manning their one picking machine. Ted was married to his Maud for sixty-four years, and at the time of writing he is eighty-four years of age with a memory as sharp as a tack despite the traumas of a recent hip replacement.

Mrs Frost as a young girl, with her sister and brother, having tea.

The tenth of October was Michaelmas, the traditional hiring and firing time for farm workers. Fairs were held across the country and men out of work went along, hoping to be taken on by farmers looking to pick up new labour. A worker hired one Michaelmas was bound to stay with his master until 10 October the following year, says Ted. It also followed that the farmer agreed to give the worker one year's employment between those two dates. All that was needed to legally seal this solemn contract was a handshake.

At the end of September the old season's strings bearing the weight of mature hop plants were cut down with the bines. Fields were left to winter with bare poles marking the aisles, still with strong wires fastened across the pole heads. Throughout winter, workers made their rounds checking wire work and the state of the wooden poles to see which needed replacing. Hard-wearing chestnut was generally favoured, as this made the longest lasting poles. Thicker tree trunks were stripped of their bark then used as 'bats' or strainers at the end of each row. Kentish woods still grow chestnuts in abundance.

This was a fairly busy time for home-dwellers who found enough to do to keep them employed in the gardens for the next couple of months. Only over Christmas and January was there a slack time and workers not employed on a regular basis went around the countryside looking for any work available. Fence repairing, building construction and roof repairs were alternative jobs on offer. Wood cutting was a necessity as most farmers and locals kept their homes warm with wood-burning stoves. There was no central heating and huge cast iron kitchen ranges with their integral hot water tanks (the only hot water in the house) and in-built ovens ate wood greedily when the weather was cold. It was common to find hop bines slung across the kitchen beams of a Kent farm house as a room decoration as they helped purify the air while adding a pleasant aroma. Hop bines are still used for these same purposes in many Kent pubs and homes today. The kitchen was the warmest place in the house and was usually the centre of family life as only in wealthier houses were there fireplaces in other rooms. Heat was controlled on the kitchen range by means of the flue, the damper, fret and a judicious use of the poker at times. It would be hard for a modern housewife to understand how to regulate the temperature of these old ranges when baking, but I can say from personal experience that it could be done with great accuracy: I have never tasted shop-bought vanilla slices or sponge cakes that came anywhere near those my mother baked in one of these ovens. Wood was kept stowed against a wall or under a lean-to to keep it dry and it was common to see a whole winter's supply of fuel stacked against the driest wall.

Planting a Hop Field

Starting with the planting of a new hop field in the 1920s: if it was a new garden being planned all the poles and wires were put up in place, first. Then the hop sets were planted 6ft apart, although it didn't matter if the alley was an extra 6 inches wide for the Butchers pattern or even 8ft

G. Turner recently went back to visit the hop huts where he used to sleep and live during the picking season.

Hop picking was fun for the children!

screw into the ground very close to the set and the strings were tied down onto these. When hop sets were planted for the Butchers style, they were planted 3ft either side of the poles, so when the stringing was done it allowed 2ft between each string, but when it was for the Umbrella style the young sets were planted very close to the poles, leaving a 6ft space between them. With 6ft between both plants and rows it meant cultivation of the sets could be done by a tractor or cart going either up and down the field or across it.

Ted Bingham

Evacuees

We were evacuees and volunteered to go down hop picking. Mum travelled on the tram from Deptford to London Bridge and poor Dad had to walk all the way, pushing the hopping box with everything in it. We went to Chambers Farm at Wallerton Street, Maidstone. The pub my parents went to was called The Blue Door then; now it's called the Raspberry Arms.

Frank Larkin

Earning for Christmas

This story goes back sixty years for me, when three or four thousands of East Enders took the August holiday they'd looked forward to all year long. People travelled to all parts of rural Kent to live in a brick or tin hut about 10ft by 10ft which would be their kitchen, dining room and bedroom: it was 'home' for the time it would take to strip the fields of their hops.

wide (for the Umbrella pattern). Our garden used the Butchers style of training hops. There was a wire across the top of the poles to steady them and a bottom wire stapled to the poles which were 12ft apart. When the top wires were stapled in place they were about 12 or 13ft above ground level and strings were tied onto it with half-hitch knots. This was done by a man walking on stilts. For the Butchers pattern there was a breast wire but this wasn't used for the Umbrella pattern which required four strings to each hill; two strings going each way across two alleys. These were pulled together with a short piece of coconut string tied about breast-high to form a square. Screw pegs were used to

The mums loved it because after four weeks or so of picking the hops they would be paid for their labour by the farmer owning the hopfields. They only earned about £20 but that was as good as winning the lottery in those days. It meant Mum could be sure the whole family had a good Christmas with all the trimmings.

C. Norman

Remembering the Huts

All our family comes from the Medway towns and were pickers. Although my own memories only go back to the fifties I have loved everything about hopping all my life and never get bored returning to the old farm. Fortunately there are several paths I can follow to get to where our huts used to be. Nothing now remains of where they were except the bases but some of the cook huts remain. I have discovered an old chalk pit in the nearby woods that contains many relics originally left in the huts by hoppers, and later dumped by the farm hands. It's like an archaeological dig down there. From about 1963 the farmer had a picking machine, but still used hand pickers to do some of the work right up until the time growing ceased on his farm.

Kevin Parry

Part of G. Turner's hop hut (on the right) and the cookhouse.

George Shrieve's first visit to the hop garden. He is the baby, aged three months, being fed by his mother in 1932.

Dolly Thirkell taking a break.

Starting Young

Hop-picking in September was a regular event in my mother's family. I went with my mother, Mrs Daisy Bonner, her two sisters, Hilda Hudson and Ethel Hudson, their four children and my granddad, Thomas Wright, who was a regular pole puller. My grandmother, Emily Wright, took her family to a farm in Wateringbury for years. They were all born in Hackney and Homerton, London, and this was not only a holiday for them to get out of London but a way to earn money as times were very hard in the late 1880s and early

1890s. My mother was the youngest of eight. In 1921 Grandmother had a stroke and died while the family were down in Kent. She was buried in Wateringbury near her beloved hop gardens so my mother had to go and live with her sisters. She was eleven years old. Mother went to work at the age of fourteen and married my dad in 1928. The family still went hop-picking, but at Mayes Farm, Paddock Wood, Kent, and that's where I made my first appearance in September 1929 at the age of one month. Granddad got a wooden apple box from the farm, scrubbed it up and put two rope handles on it. Mum lined it with flannelette and hey ho! The origin of the carry cot, in which I was warm and happy (so I was told)!

Mrs L.I. Carter (née Peggy Bonner)

The Best Holidays Ever

I remember my hopping days with great nostalgia. I've had holidays all over the Continent – Spain, Greece, Italy and Germany – but I always look back on those days when we went hopping as the very best I can remember.

Joan James

Hot Tea for Everyone

An early start was required in the hop field and it was usually very chilly at the beginning of the day. Families set off to their allocated field, mainly adults and older children first then the younger children were brought along later accompanied by members of the family carrying several large pots suspended by their handles on a long wooden pole. These were slung across between the shoulders of two people and were usually filled with hot tea for everyone. Carrying individual pots by hand was uncomfortable as they were heavy and the wire handles cut into your hands.

L. Presley

The Shrieve family at their hop hut. Those pictured include George, his dad and his uncle Arthur.

Arthur Smith's family in the hop garden. From left to right: Arthur's father, his sister Daisy, brother Michael and his mother.

Stringing the Bines

I don't know if any men still walk on stilts to do stringing now, but the firm of farmers I worked for no longer has any. All their stringing is done by using long poles now, hooking the strings onto wire loops. The worker doing the job suspends a bag from his shoulder with a very large ball of string in it. The end of the string is threaded through a small piece of looped metal fixed at the top end of a 10ft long rod and he walks along the alley, reaching up to the row of hooks threaded along the top wire. He has to twist the string on the top hook, then down to the screw peg in the ground and loop it onto

this, then up again to the next hook on the top wire.

Ted Bingham

The Pole Puller

The hop field consists of many alleyways created by rows of poles linked together by wire and string ties, up which the hops are grown in great, hanging fronds of lush green leaves with bunches of hops hanging in clusters. During the picking the high bines were cut down by the pole puller using a long pole at the end of which was mounted a scythe-like cutting blade and hook. Picking hops was a tedious task which was unpleasant if it rained. Pickers used hop sacks for protection, wearing them across their shoulders like capes to keep the worst of the rain from them.

L. Presley

Digging the Garden

Hop plants are planted in rows 6ft apart each way, giving about 1,200 plants to an acre. Sometimes crops such as mangolds are grown between the rows during the first year. Over four months, November to March, the garden was dug over with a fork with flattened prongs called a Kentish spud. This was very labour intensive so it's an expensive way to do it and most farmers now use tractors for the job. We manured the ground well during this time, using all sorts: cow, pig and horse dung, stable refuse (manure and straw) from stables in London (there were a lot of horses in

Arthur George Horne, known as 'Pats', was Debbie Wetheridge's grandfather.

London before the 1950s), wool and cotton rag waste, and fish manure from the fish markets where the women hand-gutted the fish. This was ploughed in over the winter. Around our area we dug in guano, nitrate seeds, rape dust and artificial manures over the summer using a Canterbury hoe.

George Green

A Hard Day's Work

I was born on 27 December 1914 and married a farmworker who worked on a hop farm: Grange Farm, Tonbridge. I'd never known farm work before but I suppose I accepted it. It was very hard. I went to work at eight o'clock in the morning and came home at midday, light the kitchen fire to fry bubble and squeak and have a piece of bacon with it. We had to be out in the fields again by one o'clock. We came home at five and I had to cook a proper dinner for ourselves – you always cooked enough so you could have a little bit left over for lunch the next day. Then there was the children's washing to do, bath them and get them to bed.

Alice Heskitt

Hopping Rations

Getting ready to go hopping started early for the families who, each week during the year from one September to the next, bought tins of food to add to the hopping box, such as soup, corned beef, Spam and all kinds of dry food such as rice, sugar and tea. This was because the nearest shop was three or four miles walk from the huts.

C. Norman

Arriving at the Hut

It was a steep hill to the huts. You had to pull the hopping box back in case it ran away. We'd open the hut door and give the place a good clean out. We put wood apple and orange boxes on the walls to put all our stuff away, then a curtain to hang down at the door to hide it all. We filled our palliasse and pillows with straw the farmer gave us then put the straw mattress on top. You were that high on the bed you had to help each other up. It flattened after a few nights lying on it. All our boots were lined up ready for Monday morning, the start of the picking.

Hop Picker

Five Miles to the Shops

On Saturday afternoons I walked from Grange Farm to Tonbridge, about five miles, to do my shopping. I did two lots of baking a week. I made the jam, bottled my own fruit, everything. I'd open the pantry and the boys would say 'Mum, can we have some cherries today?' or 'Can we have some pears?'

Alice Heskitt

Hop pickers relaxing over a game of cards in the evening, 1950.

Mrs Bunker, Anne and
Martin.

Hop Facts

From the time that the hop plant was introduced into England, Kent has been the principal centre of its cultivation. In 1906 out of a total of 46,722 acres in the country, Kent contained 29,296 acres, or about two thirds. In 1878 when the hop acreage of the country reached its highest point of 72,000 acres, there were 46,600 acres in Kent alone. The yield was between 7 and 9.6cwt an acre. At one time, hops were grown in 313 Kent parishes.

An extract from The Victorian History of
the County of Kent, *by George Green,*
published 1908

CHAPTER 2

Winter's Silence, Nature's Patience

Refuelling a Sikorsky helicopter at Horsham, Sussex, in 1949. The helicopter took on board fuel, compressed air and a 5 per cent DDT emulsion, which was sprayed over the hop gardens at 2 gallons per acre. (Courtesy of the Hop Farm Country Park)

This was a quiet time in the hop gardens, apart from new plants being bedded in October or November. Hops and fruit have always gone hand in hand, the sites of old orchards being ideal for growing hops. Some farmers grew fruit trees or beans to bring in a little extra profit while new hop plants were developing. Hop growing is costly to establish as it takes up land full-time. Once the hills were entrenched they remained in place for the next twenty years, so farmers were limited in what else they could do to increase their profits. 'You may plant a double row of garden beans between each row of hills; as well to yield some profit the first year, as to shelter the [hop] bud from the scorching heat of the sun,' advised 'J.A.' in The Hop Garden (1721). Bean crops were taken by horse and cart to local markets such as Faversham, Ashford and Maidstone.

Stringing the poles (courtesy of the Hop Farm Country Park).

Mr George Kendall with his daughter, Mary.

Fuggles hop plant (courtesy of the Hop Farm Country Park).

Much of the heavy farm work was done by work horses, more commonly used than tractors before the end of the war. Working with horses was satisfying but more labour-intensive than using heavy machinery. One man and his horse walked a total of eleven miles to plough one acre with a single-furrow plough. Tractors need simple, mechanical maintenance whereas horses require grooming daily, hooves need checking for cracks due to hard road work, bad shoeing or standing for long periods on wet ground. They need feeding regularly with hay, bran and linseed mash in the winter and one acre per horse of paddocking for grazing. A regularly worked horse also needs corn mixed with chaff, cut on a hand-turned chaff cutter and numerous buckets of water if kept in stabling. While some

farmers tended to neglect their farm horses' harness, dray horses on show to the public needed their tack (bridle, breast collar, reins, hames, traces etc) and horse brasses kept in good order; many hours needed to be spent cleaning leather with saddle soap and neatsfoot oil, repairing worn reins and polishing up the brassware until it gleamed. This is all work I have done myself, so I can vouch for the sore hands from pulling on linen threads, pricked fingers from the awl and needles and aching arms from turning the heavy chaff cutter. Hop-pickers remember with affection the huge farm horses used to haul hop carts around the gardens to collect the pokes for the oast. Sometimes a farmhand gave pickers lifts into local villages or towns to do their shopping. Because they were always in the public eye and a form of advertisement for their wares, breweries took pride in the breeding of their horses and well matched pairs were a common sight. Whitbreads used Shires and these amiable giants can still be seen on their former Beltring farm, now the Hop Farm Country Park. Other breeds were Suffolk Punch, Clydesdale and the lesser known Percheron. These magnificent animals are now mainly seen at horse shows, but up until the 1950s they were the kings of the road and a common sight in both country and city. Hoppers arriving at country stations looked eagerly for the horses and carts taking them to the hop farm with their belongings and the horses became firm friends to be greeted fondly on re-acquaintance each season. During the early months of the year these same animals were to be seen trudging patiently along the aisles, stopping to allow farm workers to unload fertilizer, compost or fresh hop poles along the way, clip-clopping down the country lanes into the village to deliver fresh produce or taking the family to church or the shops. The majority of former hop gardens have now changed over to other types of farming. The Kentish countryside would not be the same without its picturesque oast houses, and while some of the old oasts were demolished, many have been converted to modern dwellings, saved to enhance the Rowland Hilder-esque landscape of the county.

The New Year

Christmas and New Year saw little happening in the fields apart from maintenance work, although tools always

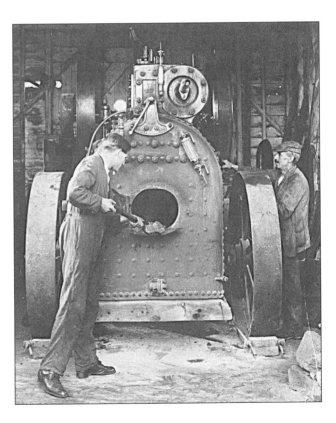

A traction engine at Whitbreads Hop Farm, Beltring, now the Hop Farm Country Park.

At the Hop Farm Country Park, formerly Whitbread's, during the winter.

needed sharpening and wooden handles checking for replacement. New, hand-made scuppets were ordered; hop presses were cleaned and put in working order; the heavy leather supporting belt required replacing after several seasons' use and working parts of machines needed checking for excessive wear. The horsehair or hessian floors in the oasts required repairing, fresh stocks of sulphur were bought in and furnaces were given a thorough overhaul.

Ted Bingham

Short Cut to Goudhurst

Going into Goudhurst meant a five-mile walk along the road, so most times we took the direct route. This meant passing the farmhouse, up a railway embankment, onto the single track railway then along the line to Smugley's Farm. If we saw a train coming we would put a penny or ha'penny on the railway line for the steam train to flatten as it passed. We'd continue through the farm, taking a footpath past the orchards on either side of the road. To the right was a large wooden barn in which was stored a stage coach or carriage, which intrigued us and frightened me as a child. (I'd heard stories of highwaymen and Dick Turpin, I suppose.) A few hundred yards on we came to Goudhurst village with the village hall and pond to the left and Burgess the butchers to the right. They made the best steak and kidney pies I've ever tasted. Then there was the forge where the horses were shod, and the grocers. The Vine public house was across the road with Weekes the bakers up the hill on the left. At the top was the church with the Bell and Star close by. Across the road from the Bell was the post office which sold sweets, stationery and other useful items, which I found strange, coming from South London – because at that time a post office was just a post office.

Bob Orris

A Converted Oast House

The Oast House in Trottiscliffe [pronounced Trossley] was converted to a dwelling in 1926 by a group of artists who valued the positioning of the long former drying room for its eastern light. It must have made an ideal studio. They got a bargain: the oast cost them a mere £60. At that stage the beams in the upper drying room chamber were only chest high and had to be raised to allow for a new ceiling. Ownership can be traced back through the original title deeds, still in existence, to when the oast was originally built.

Phil and Amanda Haselden

Films at the Village Hall

Still set among beautiful Kent countryside, the Wrotham Water Farm, Trottiscliffe, ceased hop growing many years ago and its oast house was converted to a family dwelling. It is owned by Michael Goodworth.

At Goudhurst village in later years a film show would be held at the village hall where

Phil and Amanda Haselden's converted oast house in Trottiscliffe, May 2000.

Old Round Farm is a converted oast house near Trottiscliffe.

we all sat on wooden school chairs with the projector on a table at the rear of the hall and watched flickering pictures of Roy Rogers and his horse Trigger, or the Lone Ranger and faithful Indian friend Tonto. The trips into town were a treat but it meant carrying heavy bags of provisions back to the farm and it was hard going, so we used a staff or stout stick and slung the handles of the bag on this so we could carry it between us over one shoulder.

Bob Orris

Trottiscliffe

Nestling beneath the protection of North Weald Downs is Trottiscliffe's St Peter and

St Paul's. While the hop gardens were mainly the other side of the village, this was the place of worship for farmers, hoppers and pilgrims alike who wished to attend Sunday services. The church is along the ancient Pilgrims' Way. A church has stood on this site since soon after the See of Rochester was granted the land in AD 788. The Bishop's manor house and farm is immediately next door to the church.

George Green

Schooldays in London

I attended Vauxhall School, just across the road from our flats, but it was closed for most of the war and with my skin complaint recurring, laying me up in Lambeth hospital for nine weeks, I had very little education before I was eleven years old. I moved to secondary school, barely able to read or write, but I soon made reasonable progress although I never achieved any high academic standards. Walnut Tree Walk School was in a street opposite Lambeth Walk where there was a large bomb site which was used for the making of the film *Passport to Pimlico* with Stanley Holloway and Katherine Harrison. We schoolboys found this a lot of fun and there was plenty going on to interest us. Along the far side in Lambeth Road was an emergency water tank from the war years and this doubled up in the film as a swimming pool.

Bob Orris

Tally Man

I was second tally man at Brenley Farm for Major S. Berry in the early fifties when Ted Bingham was the waggoner and tally man. Ted has lived in the Faversham area all his life working on local farms, mostly with horses.

Dr Philip W. Bowden

The Salvation Army

Salvation Army officers went to the hopfields, too. The Army gave a half-century of service to the hop-pickers, from the post war years of the 1920s to the 1960s when machines took over the job of picking hops from the bines. Whole streets

February at Syndale Hop Farm, Ospringe.

Arthur Smith's family and pet dog.

Mrs Crimins' family, with their dog sitting in Mum's lap.

in the poor areas of London fell silent during the months of August and September as their occupants gathered for a mass exodus to Kent hop farms. The Salvation Army officers went too, taking comforts such as first aid kits, Sunday school Bible tracts, spare blankets, hot water urns and refreshments. Some officers even went to London Bridge to help families with their hopping boxes onto the early morning trains, some of which started at four o'clock in the morning. Some officers were billeted with villagers or in Sunshine Lodge in Yalding, owned by the Salvation Army. The rest of the year the Lodge was used for holidays and weekend breaks for deprived people. When the hoppers broke off from their picking – mid morning, lunch time and mid afternoon – the Salvation Army officers were there ready with their tea urns to serve mugs of tea and slabs of cake to the hard-working pickers. Until the Army started going down to the fields, mothers had laid their babies nearby on sacks laid on the ground but the officers provided crèches for the youngest children. Originally these were simply hay-filled sacking used as beds, but later the Army provided large tents and folding cots. The Army also supplied hot baths on Friday or Saturday nights. These were well received, especially considering the primitive conditions of most camps. The cost was a penny per child; three children for twopence if they all belonged to the same family! The baths were made of zinc and had a metal handle at each end so were portable (they can still be bought by plasterers in some hardware stores.) Preparation was hard work, what with gathering wood for the fires to heat the water which had to be carried up to half a mile from a solitary standpipe, poured into

One of Mrs Ethel Chandler's sisters, Lou, at Seal Farm, Sevenoaks.

coppers, ladled into the baths, all the while keeping the fires burning with fresh faggots. Because of this, the same water was used by successive bathers: ladies first, children next. As well as these duties the officers held Sunday school for the children, prayer meetings for the adults and evening camp fires where everyone gathered to talk, sing and tell stories. They also ran an emergency service for coping with severe illnesses or deaths among the pickers, informing relations back in London. On one sad occasion an officer met a gipsy family pushing a pram and obviously very upset. The pram contained the body of a small child who had fallen in

The children and grandchildren of Mr and Mrs Kendall are gathered together outside their hop hut.

the river and drowned. The Army arranged for the child to be buried in Yalding churchyard in a small white coffin.

Abridged from The War Cry, *24 June 1978, supplied by Ken Perry*

A Policeman's View

I lived in Collier Street near Yalding. I'm not sure if our family had anything to do with the Golding hop but as it was developed nearby, it's quite possible. I was a policeman and regularly had dealings with the hop-pickers. I didn't like some of the things they got up to. Most of the hoppers were all right, but at the weekends the men came down and the visitors, and these were sometimes a problem. They'd come in their lorries, sometimes with stolen goods to sell in the hop fields. They got up to all sorts and so much was stolen from the local shops the owners used to put higher fronts on the counters, or wire netting, so the hoppers couldn't reach over without being seen.

Harry Golding

CHAPTER 3

February, March and April's Bud

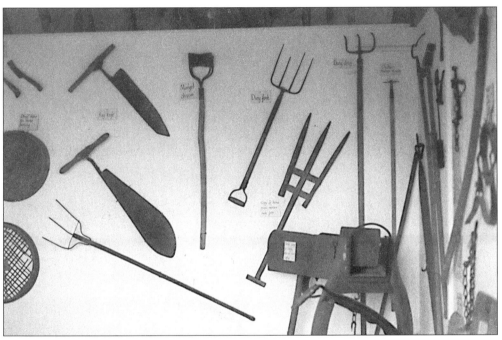

A selection of forks, hoes and other implements at the Hop Farm Country Park.

While most hop farmers planted out new sets in October, J.A. believed March to be a better time or 'the latter end of February if the weather be mild'. Each plant was built up into a hill; although these are generally only about 8 to 12 inches high nowadays, in the sixteenth century they were built knee-high with the repeated addition of compost to nourish the plant.

Stilt walkers now did their job, making their way along the aisles with bundles of pre-cut lengths of string dangling from strong leather belts. It needs brawny hips and legs to move stilts over the ground. This was usually men's work but during the war women, as well as men, did the job. Originally stilts were cut from wood but later, lighter models were made of aluminium. The stilts, some 12ft high, were strapped to the walker around his or her waist while their feet stood on projecting rests with leather toe slots to keep them in place. A walker needed to climb a ladder to put them on and got down the same way. Stilt walking was a job for

Stringing the poles (courtesy of the Hop Farm Country Park).

experts: *if a stilt stuck in the mud, or March winds blew, the walker could easily topple and it was a long way down to the ground!*

Frosts were a serious danger to newly emerging tendrils which needed protection from the worst of the icy winds. Some farmers strung netting across the top wires to prevent the worst of the frosts getting at the hops' growing tips.

Cultivating and Stringing

In March the work of cultivating would start, using different types of implements. In springtime it was harrows with a five-tine shim, or a three-wheeled cultivator.

In Kent, most hopfields were strung by one of three methods. Butchers Patent required a breast wire tied from one pole to the next and a second wire along the tops of the poles, which were 12 to 15ft high. Strings were tied from the breast wire across the aisle to the top wires of the next row. With Butchers stringing the aisles were 6ft 6in wide.

The second method was Umbrella stringing, which was used as far back as the sixteenth century and consisted of four strings from a central footing, each spread out overhead and strung across to overhead wires on either side. This method took up more room as it required a distance of 8ft between the aisles. The third method was Worcester stringing, which requires two strings reaching chest high, which then divided and were fastened overhead in a Y shape. The aisles for this method were 10ft wide.

Ted Bingham

April's Growth

During April new growth appears on the plants, and women went into the fields to 'furnish the hill', which meant picking out the weaker shoots, known as pipey bines, leaving three of four of the healthiest to flourish. This ensured strong shoots as the crown could give all its nutrients to the bines that were left. As each shoot grew, it was the women's job to twist, twiddle or twirl them up one of the strings fastened to the ground by twisted wire skewers a few inches from the hill. The women had to be careful not to break off the bine tips which were delicate and easily snapped. While beans climb in an anticlockwise direction, hops are contrary and 'follow the sun', climbing clockwise. If the weather was warm shoots could grow as much as five or six

Chambers Farm, 1949. From left to right: Peggy's father Ben, her mother, a friend called Benny and Peggy Carter (née Bonner).

At Chambers Farm, 1950. From left to right: Peggy Carter, Len (her future husband), a friend of her mother's, her father Ben, and another of her mother's friends.

inches overnight so needed daily attention. A well established and cared-for hop plant could be in use for twenty years.

Ted Bingham

Cutting the Heel

We had poles for hop training in those days. In February the men cut the heel of the hop; that's the hard root. The dirt is moved away and a slice cut into the root: this starts the new hop shoots to grow. You'd get ever so many bines from one heel but you would only keep the strongest of them as the weak ones took the strength away from the others.

We trained the new bines up at about the end of April. You put nine bines up the pole and you tied them with rushes that you picked and dried the summer before. But you had to make sure you got it all tied up! You train hops the opposite way to runner beans: anticlockwise. There could be thousands of bines to do and you had to do 900 of them tied over three times before you got 30s and I don't mind admitting, I cried many a time because, having two children with me in the field so I had to look after them, I'd be well behind the other women who'd earn more than me in a day. We'd have to put the wire and string for the bines to grow up. My husband and I would both be on stilts. He would pull the wire to the next pole while I handed him the round hook things to fix to the wire, then I used to feed the wire with these hooks to my husband.

After that was done that's when you put up the strings. A man does that job. He has the ball of string in his apron pocket and he goes along with a long hook to reach up to the wire, then down to the heel where there was a type of skewer, but bigger. All the hop bines would be wrapped round the string and you got four strings going up to the wire. Up those strings you put three bines on one string and two bines up the other. You've got to make sure the bines were close to the string because the men would go along with the tractor with a shimmer to take out the weeds and if the bines were ploughed out by mistake you wouldn't have any hops.

Alice Heskitt

The Growing Hops

In the early years of my employment on the farm I remember that in the last week of April and the first week of May the women were busy working with the men in the hop gardens, pulling out the red-coloured bines. These were called pipers and classed as no good for bearing hops. It was a well-known saying that hop training

A farrier's cart from the early twentieth century. This farrier took his trade round the country farms which needed their horses shod. One of his ports of call was Whitbread's Farm.

Mrs P. Frost's aunt, brother-in-law and niece outside the cookhouse.

The Vinall family in 1949. From left to right: Maureen's mum Daisy, Peggy Carter, Maureen's fiancée Len, and her father Ben.

started on 12 May and the foreman in charge of the trainers had to watch that all the strings to each hill were evenly matched with three young bines, each twisting clockwise around its string towards the sun. It is a fact that hops grow during the night hours; once or twice while I was cultivating in among the hops I have tied a piece of string at the head of a bine when I was about to leave for home, probably about 7 p.m., and in the morning when I returned to carry on my work that hop head could be as much as six inches higher up the string.

Ted Bingham

Mug O!

We had British Red Cross men come up the fields in the morning, calling out 'Mug, O!' for us all to have a hot drink. They used to sell sweets as well as the tea.

Pat Frost

CHAPTER 4

May and June: the Twining Bine

Throughout the months of May and June bines needed regular attention as they grew away from the strings and needed to be trained back again. Ted Bingham explained that once the plants topped 5 or 6ft, stiltwalkers had to take over from the women, taking the shoots to the top of the strings.

Farmers and workers were on constant watch for wilt which, once it attacked a crop, went through the garden like wildfire, killing off the bines. If wilt established itself unchecked in one field it could easily spread, so prompt action was imperative. Farmers go to considerable lengths to protect their crops and would be considered irresponsible if they did not do so. One untreated field could rapidly spread spores across all neighbouring hop farms and wipe out crops in the area for that season. Hop plants are at risk throughout the growing season and the only sure way to get rid of wilt once bines have been infected, is to burn the whole plant. Once bines reached the height of a man they were sprayed with a sulphur mix to kill off any wilt spores. Other less dangerous chemicals are used

Stilt-walkers training the hop bines in the 1930s (courtesy of the Hop Farm Country Park).

Syndale Farm, Ospringe. Bats have been piled up, waiting to be set as strainers to hold the wires tight at each end of the rows.

nowadays. Alice Heskitt spoke of one the worst problems of the hop grower: 'You can get a terrible hop blight which is called the red spider. If you get blight you cannot go on that hop garden at all unless you wash your wellingtons and clothes with disinfectant. You had to change your clothes and wellington boots and leave them in a tent in the field because if the blight got off the hop garden it could spread and kill all the hop plants. We'd string that diseased bine right off so nobody could get to it. We had to cut them down if they were infected, then burn them straight away before the blight travelled. Nothing more was done in the hop garden after that until the Londoners came.' She might have added the problems caused by downy mildew and verticillium wilt, which attacks plants via the root system. The usual method of eradicating these was by spraying with Bordeaux mixture, which contained up to 60 per cent copper sulphate. A packet sufficient for 10lb of fungicide spray cost 2s from the Army and Navy Stores in the 1930s.

Hop Training

It was important for women to do hop training because the men were doing other work and couldn't spare the time to train. After that you pull all the bines away from the heel and then you strip them half way up to let the air go through. When I was hop tying it made my fingers very sore. Dreadful. It really takes the skin off the back of your fingers. You could get quite bad cuts on the palms of you hands, too. But when we were stripping the bines we always wore gloves. That's why we used to ask everybody for old gloves. Some farmers didn't bother to strip the bines, but our boss always did. Hop bines grow right down with the thick leaves. It would be like a bush. That's why you have to strip them so the air can get right through.

Alice Heskitt

An Old Saying

An old saying is that the bines have to have grown over the top of the wire by June 21, midsummer. That gives you an idea when the hops are ready; not actually the hops, but the bines. If they're not, it's going to be a late hop-picking.

Ted Bingham

Hook Green Farm

We went to Beech Farm, Marden, to do our picking but they finished with Londoners and took students on for machines in 1957 and after that my husband and I got married – in 1959. Then we found another farm, Hook Green at Lamberhurst. When we first went there we didn't know what hit us. We were still in huts but we had Primus stoves to cook on and our own mattress for the bed. Quite different from the first farm. We loved it and stayed on this farm for thirteen years. While we were there I did hop training; that was in May to train the hop bines up the strings for September.

Mr and Mrs Andrews

Whitbreads are famous for their matched Shire greys. Seven of them are seen here on parade at the company's hop farm (now the Hop Farm Country Park).

Mark Streak, Sylvia Wheeler and family.

Plumford Farm

Plumford Farm lies south of Faversham, close to the hamlet of Painters Forstal. It has been run by the Elworthy family for several years. As far as I can make out, my gran, Emily Parry, went hopping there from the early 1930s. In fact she went every year until the farm stopped production in 1968. She was on the farm when the Second World War broke out. My gran had eight children, all of whom went hop-picking with her at one time or another, later taking their own families with them – including her son George (my father) and his wife Nellie (my mother). We would all travel to Faversham by lorry, usually Pilcher's coal lorry, from Gran's in West Street, Gillingham. Weeks of preparation went into this exercise. Wooden stools were made by the family and we wore rubber aprons to protect our clothing. The journey down was always memorable and from the early fifties, when I was a lad, I loved it.

Kevin Parry

Working Holiday

Families went down to have a working holiday and to earn extra money for Christmas etc., but our mum would not have gone anywhere else for her annual holiday. She loved hopping and looked forward to it, buying food throughout the year to take with her.

Maureen Vinall, née Jenkins

Earthing Up

In June the hops used to be earthed up; by this I mean a plough pulled by a pair of horses was used to push fine soil up either side of the hills. None of these traditional jobs are done now, so I'd imagine the ground gets almost as hard as our public roads. The only time you will see a tractor in a hop garden now is when the bines are being washed and when the bottom leaves are being sprayed. This treatment causes them to be burnt because a chemical substance is added to the water. While this operation is being done only two nozzles each side of the washers are used, and to stop the spray from drifting across too far, a coarse spray is set.

Ted Bingham

Goose Green Farm

My granny Underwood had been going to Goose Green Farm since 1918 and my mum has been hopping since she was two years old and she's eighty-eight, now.

Pat Cole

Scrumping

In telling you about the years of 1922 to 1928 I'm talking about the years I worked on the farm. The rules which referred to the picking and the behaviour of the pickers were printed on the back of the tally card and the person in charge of the tally basket had one of his own, so each

Pat Cole (left), aged eleven, with her mother, Mavis and Billy at Goose Green Farm, Hadlow, near Tonbridge, in 1950.

Granny Underwood in her black hat, with a friend, Grace Hoseby, at Goose Green Farm in the 1920s or 1930s.

only paid a penny per bushel for all the hops they had picked that season, then they were sent home and banned from picking for the rest of their lives.

Ted Bingham

The Red Cross Hut

At the end of the day most of the children used to go to the big hut on the cornfield and have a cup of Oxo and a board game for a penny. This was run by the British Red Cross. I was the youngest of five girls and we all went hopping. Mum and Dad had two weeks' holiday with us at the hop fields, then they would leave us with our aunts and uncles who were down there and they would look after us while our parents went back home to work. But Mum and Dad came down at the weekends, still. We used to pick in their bin for them. We also used to sub, but one year we had no money because we had subbed it all.

Pat Frost

family knew the rules and because they were there, they had to be obeyed. One particular case comes back to my mind: A family with three sons between twelve and eighteen years old were caught stealing apples. The first time they were given a very strong warning. Two days later they got careless and were caught again. This time the employer took a police officer and they went to the family's hut with the hospital charity box; they were told they either put five pounds in the box or there would be a court case. But it didn't matter which they did because their mum was

All Cousins Together

My cousins are Pat Carpenter, Beat, Ivy, Sheila, Eileen, Kenny, Dennis and Doreen. We all went hopping together. Aunt Beat and Uncle Jim had come for years. Uncle Jim was a pole puller for our set. Our huts were made of tin and were all white-washed inside. There was a dresser for all the crockery. It was really cosy, especially with the glow of the tin lamps – there was a red one and a green one. We used to look forward to seeing the same people every year. As the years went by we watched each of us grow up. Auntie Ivy and Uncle Jim Kemp and family went to Seal Chart Farm.

Pat and George Cole

Stoves and Oil Lamps

During the winter my father made us a large hopping box which converted to a table. It held all the groceries, pots and pans inside it for when we were travelling down to Kent and we sat at it for our evening meals in our hop hut. It was a wonderfully simple arrangement. Cooking was done either on a fire in the field outside, or in the cook house, which was a room with three gas cookers with slot meters shared by about a dozen families. For our morning tea, my mother had her own little oil stove in our

hut. Strangely, I can't even remember anyone causing a fire with the oil lamps or stoves in the wooden buildings.

Rita Game

Training the Bines

About thirty women were employed for hop training in our garden and this would carry on until the second week in June. By then the bine's head would normally be well out of reach of the women so they were given hazel sticks with a short branch making a 'V' shape at the top of it, so this gave the ladies a longer reach so they could turn the head of the bine around the string. Once the bines had reached the top of the strings the ladies had to strip the leaves off the lower part of

Three generations of the Larkin family outside their hop hut.

John Clinch's Syndale Farm hop garden in winter. The poles are tightly strung with wires, ready for the next season's hops.

the stems, leaving just one pair on below the breast wire, or the band string if it was where there were four to a hill.

Ted Bingham

Lolly Money

Children did sometimes pick hops. They would be given a separate sack or bucket to pick into. Their reward was usually a few pence for lolly money. This would be spent on sweets brought round the hop field by the lolly man who carried a tray of sweets and goodies through the field. He called out, 'Lolly! Lolly!' and was echoed by many children anxious to catch up with him before he left the area.

L. Presley

Strikes

In the years between 1922 and 1928 several strikes occurred in the hop gardens. This was because the pickers living in the hop huts were worried about the prices being paid for a six-bushel tally and they wanted to know how much it would be. Some of the strikers were aggressive but if they threatened any of the home pickers who were picking in the gardens and didn't want to join in the strike, or if they tipped any of the pickers' baskets of hops over deliberately, they lost a bushel or a tally off their own hop count and it was added to the victim's tally. But then most of the strikers were polite and just asked the home pickers to stop and support their strike. How the strikers were treated depended on how rude or unpleasant the strangers were to the home pickers.

Ted Bingham

Setting Up Home

Once on the farm the various members of our family would set things up to make the place comfortable. We cooked our meals on open fires and faggots (bundles of firewood) were delivered to each hut by horse and cart. Straw for our bedding was also delivered. During the picking season our rubbish was put into open 45-gallon drums and collected in the same wagon for disposal. If it rained we could use the shared cook houses. These consisted of six-post structures with corrugated tin roofs. Our original huts were made of wood, tarred on the outside, but later the farmer built breeze-block and cement screed huts which were much more comfortable and weatherproof. Lighting was provided by paraffin lamps. Our food was very basic: cheese or corned beef

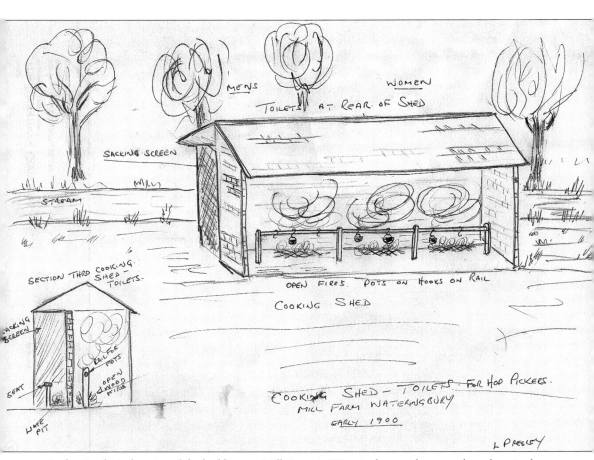

Lesley Presley's drawing of the buildings at Mill Farm in Wateringbury as he remembers them in the early twentieth century. The toilets backed onto the cooking shed, facing the stream.

The Pearly Kings and Queens gather at Rochester.

Tom Johnson, Pearly King of Bow Bells, with a City of London policeman.

sandwiches for lunch with stewed tea in flasks to drink at the hop fields.

Kevin Parry

Strict Timetables

I can remember hop picking in 1924 when I was twelve years of age. That year the farmer was surprised with a very good crop of a certain variety of apples and the women who lived at the farm cottages spent some days picking apples, so I was left to pick hops at my mother's tally on my own. One day the farmer came out into the garden and asked the tallyman how many bushels of hops I'd picked. When he was told I had picked twelve bushels he gave me half-a-crown [2s 6d] for my work. In the end, it turned out that this was the price paid for a tally of six bushels that year, so I had been given only half pay. At this farm there were three tallies of 60-bushel baskets so this allowed work for three tally men and fifteen bin men. First, No. 1 tally man called all the pickers to work at 7 a.m. Nobody was permitted to start picking hops before then. The hop pickers' day was very organized. At 10 a.m. the first measure was taken. The hops were shot into hop pokes which each held about 12 bushels. This time round, only tallies of 6 bushels were taken. About 11.30 a.m. No. 1 tally man would shout 'Load Light!' This meant not to pull down more bines than could be picked before 12 p.m. At noon time he called to the pickers to clear up around their bins. Nobody was allowed to pick between 12 p.m. and 1 p.m. – this was everyone's dinner time. At 1 p.m. No. 1 tally man called the pickers back to work. All three tally men would start about 11.45 a.m., taking in the rest of the

morning's picking. In the afternoon at about 2.30 p.m. all the tally men would go around again, taking and recording only full baskets. This meant only measures of six bushels were being taken, not half baskets. At 4.30 p.m. 'Clear up!' was called with a short break for tea, then about 4.45 p.m. they started again, taking and recording the rest of the afternoon's pickings.

Ted Bingham

The Hoppers' Special

We left home at 2 a.m. to catch the Milk Train, or Hoppers' Special, to Goudhurst. It was usually raining and the train stopped at all the little stations on the way down, dropping off churns of milk for the villages. Father made a wooden box on wheels. It had two flaps for doors because once we got down to the hop huts it was turned on its side and used as a larder. One day this box was so overloaded it broke down on the way to London Bridge station and we had to gather everything up out of the road and somehow push it all onto the train. It was all right once we were at Goudhurst because farm carts from Smuggley's Farm came to meet the hoppers at the station. The Hoppers' Special ran at night because there wasn't much traffic on the railway then.

Tom Johnson

CHAPTER 5

July and August: the Final Thrust

Checking on the growth rate of the bines at Beltring, Paddock Wood, in the early 1930s (courtesy of the Hop Farm Country Park).

Although the bine itself grows to 15ft high, only the cones are used from the whole plant. The bin man's hook was very similar in shape and size to a medieval halberd, and I believe it is possible that either halberds developed from hop hooks, or maybe it was a halberd that a medieval hop puller used to hook down his bine when he found he couldn't reach it on the top wires.

By July and August growers were aware of the current value of their hop crops. The price was affected by a number of factors, not the least of which was whether breweries were buying foreign hops rather than those from English gardens. Some brewers offset their costs by purchasing from abroad. Weather was another problem affecting prices: severe frosts, strong winds or too much rain were all detrimental to the growth of the bines and their crops. A severe influx of blight could wipe out several hop gardens' crops in an area if it wasn't brought under speedy control. All these natural disasters brought about a shortage of hops and prices rose accordingly. If the hops were small because of poor weather it meant pickers had to gather more hops to fill their bushel baskets and

Liz and Jim Tibbott, Joyce Rogers' parents, picking at their bin.

it was harder work for less pay, so when brewers imported hops there was a general outcry from pickers, who went on strike. There have been several occasions of this, when Kentish pickers got together and marched on London to demand that only English hops were used in English beer and that hoppers were paid fairly for their efforts.

Getting the Letter

My gran would get her letter from Plumford Farm during July each year, asking her to confirm how many huts she wanted. (It was usually three.) Each hut would be allocated a row of hops to pick per section. She would usually visit the hop gardens between Whitsun and September to wallpaper or paint the interior of our huts, using distemper, and also to visit her sister-in-law, Ada Godden, who spent the spring and summertime on the farm doing the hop training.

Kevin Parry

Uncertain Wages

You never knew what you were going to be paid per bushel because this depended on the size of the hops. In a dry summer the hops were smaller than in a wet one. So you didn't know how much pay you had to come until the end of the picking time.

John Meinke

Beds in the Hop Huts

Our bed in the hop hut was made from branches laid side by side and nailed to a

Mr Rule trims the wick of his Aladdin paraffin lamp in his hop hut.

frame, then a layer of straw on top of that and Mother used to take down a quilt cover which she filled with straw and lay it across the bed to sleep on. We had our own fireplaces outside the huts but on rainy days we cooked in a larger hut called the cook house. The farmer delivered faggots every day for our fires. Sometimes he brought a bit of coal or coke because the faggots soon burned through and it was hard to keep the fire going without a bit of coal at the heart of it. I think Smuggley's Farm was owned by Whitehead and Coleman. It was two miles out of Goudhurst village across the fields.

Tom Johnson

Eager Preparations

Around the last week of August, London children would be stopping their postman and asking 'Have you got our hopping letter, please?' This was the same all over the East End. What they were hoping to be given was a letter from the farmer telling the mums when to come down to Kent to pick the hops. Once the letters arrived the mums would contact the farmer, telling him they would be down on the Friday as this would give them the weekend to get their huts ready to live in for the next month or so. Pots, pans, china, towels etc. and all the food that had been saved had to be collected together, then Dad would go down to Chrisp Street market and borrow a big wheelbarrow. Once this was home it was loaded with all the stuff Mum had got ready for the hop fields. At about 4 a.m. Dad would put three small children on top of all the luggage then, with Dad pushing the barrow, we walked from Poplar all the way to London Bridge to catch the milk train to Cranbrook. We'd meet up with about 150 other families all going hopping. Dad made sure of the right train, then lots of children ran through the platform gates to the train; this was because many families couldn't afford the fares for all the children so they'd hide some of them once they were on board. We'd help load our luggage on the train then Dad had to return the barrow to the market in case the owner missed it. The train pulled away and after about $1\frac{1}{2}$ hours we pulled into Cranbrook station. Just a few seconds before the train stopped we children were out of the train doors and running across a nearby field where we'd wait for Mum to pick us up. We had to do this because Mum had no tickets for us. Waiting for us outside the station was the farmer's big four-wheeled wagon pulled by two very large horses which he'd sent to collect all his hop-pickers. Everything was loaded onto the wagon, everyone got on, sitting on anything that was handy then we were off to the farm where everyone was dropped off at the huts.

C. Norman

Like Country Kids

We children always wanted to do the shopping, going up to the village, walking along the lanes, playing about with sticks and walking in our wellingtons. We really thought we were country kids until we got to the shops. They put extra wood on the counter to make it high so we couldn't pinch anything; they didn't trust the Londoners and being in the war everything was rationed as things were in short supply. We hoppers had to queue for everything but the locals went round to the shops' back doors and got theirs straight away.

Jean Pilbeam

Packing

In early August the hopping box was cleaned up (we used it for collecting coke from Vauxhall or Nine Elms gasworks the rest of the year) and the packing started. Hopping pots, hanging hooks, enamel mugs and plates, pie and mash knives and forks (they always had black handles), jumble sale pullovers and jumpers. 'They'll

be all right for work' was a favourite saying of Mum's.

Bob Orris

Tally Baskets

Talking about the old cane tally baskets (which held 6 bushels of hops each if they were filled to the top rim of it) – these measuring baskets were done away with about 1948 on our farm and six new metal ones were bought to replace them. Only these new ones could hold seven bushels each. By this time one of the tallyings had

Laura Warner aged five in 1937 (courtesy of Mrs Rule).

These hop huts at Whitbreads were later swept away in a storm when the nearby River Medway flooded (courtesy of the Hop Farm Country Park).

One of the cookhouses at Whitbreads farm before it was swept away by the flood (courtesy of the Hop Farm Country Park).

Round the camp fire after a day's picking at Whitbreads Hop Farm (courtesy of the Hop Farm Country Park).

been cut out, leaving only two, and the measurers had three measuring bins each, so when the measuring of the hops was taking place they had to be moved around the tally. Luckily they were light so were very easy to move.

Ted Bingham

Ankle Deep in Mud

In 1946 we arrived at the farm in the early hours of the morning during heavy rain. The track up to our hut was ankle deep in mud. Having arrived at the hut, Mum got in a panic because she had lost her ration book.

Michael Jenkins

Fetching Water

Our huts were just off the Common. They were narrow but went from front to back. The water supply was from a standpipe on the Common so collecting and fetching water was a great meeting place for us kids, with much soaking and muddy clothes.

Bob Orris

Lunchtime

At lunchtimes the hooter sounded for a break. The families ate their sandwiches and drank tea served from the large pots. These pots were brought fresh from the cook huts by family members. A hot drink on a chilly day – wonderful! During the day sounds of

Whitbreads often put on a party for their hop-pickers (courtesy of the Hop Farm Country Park).

families talking and laughing with each other were often accompanied by singing some of the old songs. There were no radios or televisions in those days but people were able to make their own amusements.

L. Presley

The Last Day

The last day everything was packed. Our mothers would go down to the farm manager's house for their pay. Some of my aunts had subbed (or borrowed) most of their pay during the four weeks so had little to come, but that didn't matter as to them, and to us it was considered more of a holiday

than a job. If my brother and I had worked well we were rewarded with a ten shilling note and we could not wait to get home to spend it. I remember buying my first all china doll for 9s 6d from my pay – I got it from the Dolls' Hospital in Stratford High Street – and longing for the year to pass quickly so we could go hopping again.

Rita Game

Pea Shooter Battles

At the farm there were many things to keep us children happy when not in the hop fields. Being September everything was in abundance: blackberries, apples, cobnuts, damsons and mushrooms as big as teaplates. There were tall, hollow reeds we could make into whistles or pea shooters. Our ammo was a plentiful supply of hard, green, unripe elderberries. During the slack times around the bin my brothers Jimmy, Charlie and myself would have pea shooter battles which drove Mum mad. During the Blitz we had three families from the upper floors of Vauxhall buildings sleeping in our flat which had only two bedrooms, one living room, a long passageway, a scullery and one bathroom.

Bob Orris

Walking through London

Our families continued to go every year to Mayes Farm in Paddock Wood with more children being added to the family and coming with us, including my sister Joyce, born in 1933, and my brother Benny, born 1936. Every year around August our house was full of excitement as we were starting to pack the 'Big Box' with the wheels on. This box stood in the bedroom with a cloth over it all year, doubling as a dressing table most of the time. It always amazed us how much went into this box. There were clothes, wellingtons, cooking utensils, buckets and bowls, crockery, cutlery, bedding and pillows as well as medicines. All these things were necessary for our holiday on the hop farm. Then when the day arrived to go we got up early and set off to catch the Milk Train from London Bridge to Paddock Wood. It was a very long walk from Homerton especially for the older children, but the young ones had rides on the hopping boxes or on Dad's shoulders as most of the dads walked with us to London Bridge, then back

again to go to work. As we walked through Mare Street, Bethnal Green, Shoreditch and Liverpool Street, then over the River Thames to London Bridge, more hop-pickers came along to join us. It was like the Pied Piper. Everyone was happy to be going to Kent for the hop-picking. All the boxes were loaded into the guard's van, then we were off!

Mrs L.I. (Peggy) Carter

The Arrival

When we arrived at the huts Mum had a collection for the wagon driver and this came to about £5, which was a lot of money to him. We all settled in our same huts which in some cases may have been used by the family for ten or more years. The mums sorted out their stuff and started on making the huts more like home, which it was to be for the next few weeks. The farmer unloaded about 200 bundles of long thin sticks, or faggots, and each mum took twenty bundles each to lay on the hut floors, all along one side. On top of the faggots they laid straw until it was about a foot thick and on top of the straw they made up one big bed; Mum and the girls down one side and the boys on the other. The oil stoves were filled with paraffin as these were needed to keep the hut warm at night as it could get very cold, then the paraffin lamp was filled so we'd have light at night. The few men who were there made cooking fireplaces for each hut, about 10ft away. These each needed two 5ft stakes in the ground with a stake across the top, nailed at each end so that they looked like door frames. From the horizontal stakes were hung wire hooks from which the mums hung the cooking pots and, boy, the flavour

Hop Picking in Kent

The Stilt Walker

of the food they cooked was fantastic! It was the children's job to collect the firewood. When all this was done we had the rest of the weekend to get everything ready for Monday and our first walk to the hopfield to start picking.

C. Norman

The Measurer

Returning to the hop huts was the best part of the day. A hooter signalled finishing time. Families gathered their belongings leaving the bin standing in a folded position with A-frames folded and handles close together. The bins were emptied during the day by the Measurer. He used a basket to dip the hops out of the bin into a larger basket for later transfer into sacks called pokes. The measure was recorded in bushels which were counted for each family and the quantity entered in the tally book, the tally being credited to the family using that particular bin. Pickers received payment against the amounts picked, either weekly or as agreed with the farm's agent.

L. Presley

Black Market

During the war we always got extra rations, being farm workers. I used to put up some of the soldiers' wives. Then if the soldiers were down for the weekend they used to stay at my place as well. A lot of fiddling went on in wartime: we got very friendly with this Army cook and he used to bring us cheese, meat, sugar, jam, everything. There was one soldier who stayed with us; he was the most marvellous artist. He'd sit with my boy on his knee and draw wonderful pictures; he could write a letter at the same time! He would write a letter to his wife with his right hand while he was drawing with his left.

Alice Heskitt

Cheesy Feet

Our beds were made from large sacks stuffed with straw and laid on trestle frames supplied by the farmer. All the children in our family, whatever their ages, would have one hut to sleep in; boys one end of the bed, girls the other, cheesy feet and all. We children were required to pick hops each morning and then run any errands the grown-ups needed, before we were allowed off to play. Errands may mean going to the village shop to collect anything from a box of matches to a can of paraffin. Considering it was about one mile from the huts to the village, heavy paraffin was not a popular errand, especially as there was a very steep track called Stoney Alley to negotiate on the way.

Kevin Parry

Policing the Hop Fields

The police usually chose unmarried policemen to go down to Kent on hop duty because we were down there for nearly three months at a time: we were sent down one month before hop picking was due to start so the locals got to know us, and us them, then we had to stay for a month or so afterwards to clear up any problems. I'd only been married a few months, but they sent me down anyway.

Harry Golding

Filling the Bins

Everyone was given a drift or aisle, about 500 yards long. Your bin was placed at the end of the drift and we pulled down the bines from the overhead wires in our drift. We picked hops into a canvas bin nailed onto a wooden frame, about 10ft long and 5ft wide. There would be maybe three or four people each side of the bin all picking off the one bine and dropping the hops into the bin. We each had to pull our own bine and clear the hops off it. When we'd pulled down the twenty-four bines nearest to us we had to get each end of the bin,

pick it up and carry it to the next twenty-four bines, then you carried on doing this all the way down the drift. This was done every day, with a new drift once the old one was cleared, until the whole field was stripped. Then we'd move on to the next field.

C. Norman

Starting Young

I went hopping from the age of three but can only remember from the age of seven. Each year I helped my mum to pack all the necessary things we would need for the few weeks we were going to spend in the hopfields. It all went into the tea chest which was our hopping box and we would start to do this at the end of July. Each family had a hut to themselves and I used to share the hut we had with Mum, Nan and two brothers. The hut itself was divided into two sections by a wooden partition. All the farmer supplied us with was a bavin, which was a bundle of sticks, and some straw. My mum would put the straw on the floor and then the bavins would go in front of it so the straw wouldn't go all over the place. We had to get water in a billy can from a stream at the back of the huts. The first day Mr Grey would be waiting. We would walk across two meadows to reach the hop garden. We took with us the food for the day, the billy can of water and one bavin. The day would normally end at five o'clock when we would have to walk back across the meadows to the hut, light a fire and Mum cooked the evening meal.

Stan Dalton

A 1920s Fowler 7hp traction engine at Beltring (courtesy of the Hop Farm Country Park).

A Cold Shower

At six in the morning we would clamber aboard the cart which was pulled by a tractor and away we went at a slow, ambling pace to the hop fields. The late risers were picked up at eight and brought back two hours later than us in the afternoons. The mornings were usually crisp and often misty, clearing as the sun warmed the day. The first bines were always wet from dew or rain and when the pole pullers brought the bines down everyone in the vicinity got a cold shower. Hop bins were set up at the end of the hop rows and the adults and older children filled up bushel baskets and tipped them into the bins. It took quite a lot of baskets to fill a bin. At the end of each working day a tallyman came round, the bins were emptied and the pickers paid. Being a youngster at the time I didn't take a lot of notice of this procedure; there were more exciting things to see and do.

Maureen E. White

Deliveries in the Fields

Once picking started the farmer employed some of the men from the labour force to drive tractors with trailers to carry the pokes and to pull bines for the pickers. My father had these jobs on several occasions over the years. During our day's picking, various visitors came and went round the fields. We were able to buy things from the Co-op milkman and Co-op baker's van. The district nurse came. She called out with humour 'Bring out your dead!' while on Sundays the vicar ran a Sunday school for the children. It would take the workers about five weeks to pick all the hop gardens, which stretched right up the valley. Our family worked five and a half days a week and during the weekends our uncles, cousins and friends came down to visit us, giving them a day out. Hops were collected twice every day and once on Saturdays. They were taken to the oast house on White Hill to be dried. The oast has now been converted into a dwelling house.

Kevin Parry

Remington Farm

Our family went hopping at Remington Farm, Goudhurst, with my nan. In another hut were my mum's friends, Mr and Mrs Micklewhite. They wallpapered their hut and it was always very comfortable. They didn't bother with faggot beds like the other hoppers; instead, they took their own mattress down with them. Their nephew was Michael (Micklewhite) Caine, the film star. I really loved going down hopping.

Pauline Hart (née Newman)

London Weekenders

Mostly, the hoppers were no problem as we didn't take too much notice of the smaller crimes such as poaching and scrumping. Our main problem was the weekenders coming down from London and the difficulties of general control with hundreds of people turning up in a small village and only a couple of policemen to deal with them. There was a place called Seven Mile Lane, and it was known as the Escape Route because this was the way thieves came down – and got away – in their lorries with stolen

The Larkin family at Chambers Farm.

property they'd try to sell to the folk in the hop fields. One difficult year was 1953 when it was Her Majesty the Queen's Coronation and police were drafted in from all over the country to help with crowd control in London. When the Kent contingent were called, the others called out 'Here come the hop-pickers!'

Harry Golding

CHAPTER 6

September: Happy Hopping – Remember?

Emily Parry (left) with her sister-in-law, Ada Godden, who regularly went hop training before also helping at the picking.

By early August postcards or letters were sent from Kent's hop farms to the 40,000-strong army of pickers in and around London, all eagerly awaiting news that the hopping season was about to begin and that their family could go on their cherished annual holidays. By September the hoppers were on the move; only a trickle at first, as those privileged to travel early to their hop farms went down to paint, paper and decorate their hop huts ready for the family's imminent arrival. By the first week in September the trickle became a flood as all roads leading to London Bridge station were blocked with families trundling their tea-chest-and-pram-wheeled 'opping boxes piled high with paraffin lamps, enamel washbowls, Valor stoves and everything else a regular hopper needed for three to six weeks' working holiday. Hoppers' Special trains waited on the platforms, steam huffing from smokestacks, as families queued to *show their tickets for inspection. It must have been an impossible task to check these properly while children ran up and down in excitement and eager hoppers tried to push their way through the barriers, keen to find the best seats in the carriages. Many children got through without a ticket and were hidden under the seats behind their mum's long skirts or in the luggage racks. At the same time dozens of lorries waited in back streets as families clubbed together to afford transport down to their hop garden where they occupied huts next to their neighbours from home.*

Loading the Lorry

As children we always teased our mums trying to climb into the back of the lorry on the day we were actually going hopping. It was great fun loading the lorry with bedding, bikes, food, and a chair was always kept available for Mum to sit on. Most of the children sat looking out of the back and waving to everyone as we passed. My dad got upset when it came round to hopping time because he'd be left behind and it was always known as 'Dad has the murr'.

Maureen Vinall

Earning Your Ice Cream

While the grow-ups were picking hops, heads down, fingers flying, there was plenty of chatting and laughter going on and that was our clue to go off and explore the woods and fields around us. They were halcyon days and I remember well the intoxicating feeling of freedom. When I was seven or eight an ice cream cart came round the hop fields and I asked my Aunt Mag if I could

have a wafer. 'Yes,' she said, 'but you'll have to earn it. Go and find how much it costs.' Off I went at a run and was soon back. 'Sixpence,' I said. 'In that case you can have one, but you'll have to pick hops and fill a bushel basket to earn it.' I was happy with that and when I had finished my wafer of ice cream I set to and laboriously filled a basket. When I told me aunt the ice cream man would be coming round every day she said 'In that case you will have to fill a bushel basket with hops each day if you want to earn sixpence.' It wasn't until years later that it dawned on me the lesson my aunt was trying to teach me.

Maureen E. White

Stabbings

We lived at Collier Street near Yalding. While I was on police duty during the hop-picking season two licensees at two different pubs in the area were stabbed by hop pickers in one night.

Harry Golding

Good for the Kids

Many of the hoppers were costermongers and they came back to London after their fortnight's hop-picking holiday looking fit from their time in the country. They used their horses and carts to take down everything they needed for their holiday. They took their grandmas too. At the end of the hopping the farmer would ask them 'Will you be back next year?' and put their names down to book their places. It was something good for the kids to do as they were expected to pick as well, but they also had all the fun of the country, jumping into ponds for a swim and running down the fields to explore the countryside.

Freda Blois

A Hut Like a Palace

The man in the next hut had it looking immaculate! There was a carpet on the floor, curtains at the window, drapes round his bed and it was so beautifully decorated it looked like Buckingham Palace. We lived in a house in Hankey Place, which was in a rough area and when we were bombed out Dad went off to find us somewhere safer to live. He came across a house in a much nicer area nearby – 26 Falmouth Road – so he moved us in and asked the council if we could pay rent for there instead of Hankey Place. They agreed. The house belonged to the Trinity Trust Foundation. My dad always claimed he was the first squatter in London. One of my friends didn't like to tell people she came from Hankey Place, so she used to walk through from Falmouth Road and pretend to people that she came from there instead.

Pauline Hart (née Newman)

Stuck in the Mud

One day when it was very muddy, all the pickers were returning from the hop garden to the huts when Aunt Maud got stuck in the mud and couldn't move. Everyone thought it

A children's tea party at the Whitbreads hop festival, c. 1940 (courtesy of the Hop Farm Country Park).

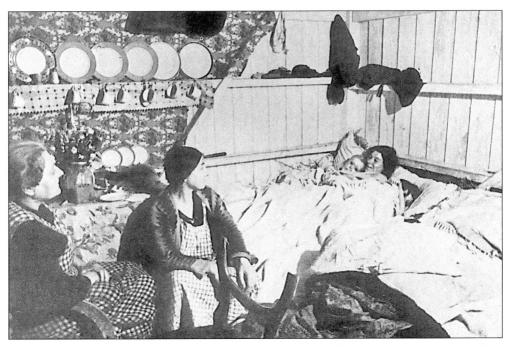

There was not much room in a hop hut, but hoppers were always willing to adapt (courtesy of the Hop Farm Country Park).

was funny, particularly when her son shouted it was because she was 'too bleeding fat!' I remember everyone joining in, singing songs played on the radio while we were picking. When the pole puller shouted 'All to dinner!' the children were sent to collect wood for lighting the fire to boil the old black kettle for tea. We used to argue over who was to carry the kettle because whoever did ended up with black legs. One weekend our cousin came to stay and we were in hysterics when she got ready for bed in her baby-doll pyjamas! Everyone slept in the same wooden bed which was divided by separate bedding. My brother refused to 'sleep in the same bed with all those women' and slept on the old trunk we'd used to transport our things down to Kent.

Maureen Vinall

Hops Ready!

When the hop-picking started we picked for about two hours until a voice was heard shouting 'Hops ready!' and all the families had to clear their bins of twigs and leaves before the measurer came with his basket. He'd dip this into a hop bin and scoop out a bushel full, which the tally lady marked down in her book against our name. This was tipped into large sacks held open by another man who shouted out 'One! Two! Three!…' counting the bushels until all tops were collected from the bin. Then the lady would add the tally up and it would be written in her book. At the end of the hop-picking all the bushels you had picked were added up in the tally book and then we got paid according to how many bushels we'd picked. This may be £20 or

Florrie Stanley with a full bushel basket of hops. Christine George is Florrie's granddaughter and now works for Shepherd Neame brewery.

£30, which was a lot of money in those days.

C. Norman

Dad's Visits

When Dad was not down for his annual fortnight holiday he would come for the weekend and my mum and I walked into Cranbrook to meet him. We went shopping in the International Home Stores and visited the sweet shop to buy what we called 'Nutty Nutty' chocolate bars. Then we'd visit the pub – The Old House at Home – before walking the mile back to the farm with all our shopping on the pushchair. On

the way Dad would eat the cheese Mum had bought at the stores.

Maureen Vinall

Stampeding Cows

One of the jobs I was given to do in the hopfields was to fetch water from a nearby brook. This was used to brew the tea. I took a large enamel jug which had to be carried to the far end of the next field. Once the jug was filled it was very heavy and I would walk across the field as fast as I could to the wooden stile. Climbing over was no easy task and by the time I arrived back the jug was nearly half empty and I would be sent back for another one. On one particular journey to fetch water the farmer had put a herd of cows in the top end of the field. I had not noticed them on the way to the brook, but by the time I was coming back they had moved further down field. I was hurrying back with my heavy load when the cows started to run towards me. I panicked and started to run too. The cows ran faster, which really scared me. I screamed and ran for the stile as fast as I could, all the while yelling for my aunt. She came running and reached the stile just as I tumbled over it. She said 'You silly moo; the cows are harmless. They won't hurt you.' Then she asked where the jug was and I explained I had dropped it in the field. Aunt Mag was a bit annoyed with me as she'd thought I'd fallen and hurt myself. Nevertheless she took my hand and we went off to retrieve the jug and refill it. She said, 'Look at the cows; they're not interested in you at all. There was nothing to be scared of.' We filled the jug again and once more set off across the field. All was fine until we got two-thirds of the way then suddenly the cows

A selection of hop tokens from Kent's hop gardens (courtesy of the Hop Farm Country Park).

charged. 'Run!' shouted my aunt Mag, and I didn't need telling twice. We made it to the stile and were over in quick time and all that was left in the bottom of the jug was about an inch of water. One of the older lads had the job of fetching the water from then on.

Maureen E. White

An Adventurous Ride

My first visit to Wateringbury, Kent, was in September 1925. We went hop-picking at Fremlin's Mill Farm when I was six weeks old. This probably accounts for my great affinity with Wateringbury and the hop fields where I spent about five weeks each year with my family: mother, brother and sister. Dad cycled down from London to join us each weekend (about forty miles). My last visit was in 1938. I took great delight in sleeping fully clothed, lying on top of the cart the night before we left London, so I was already in place for an early morning start. The ride to the hop fields was always an adventure which sometimes required the adults to get off the lorry and push it up some of the steeper hills. The old lorries were not so reliable.

L.G. Presley

Tractor Accident

One day all the children were playing on a tractor trailer. A little boy (a home-dweller) unscrewed the leg which secured the tractor and as it was tipping up, my brother Ted rescued the boy's younger sister who was underneath. Ted ended up with a broken leg because the trailer landed on him and when his wellingtons were removed our Mum hit him because he had dirty feet.

Maureen Vinall

It Always Rained

I can never remember the time when it wasn't raining on our arrival at the farm. It was the task of the children to fill the mattresses with straw and the pillowcases with hay for our beds. My mother would unpack the freshly-laundered sheets and blankets and make up the beds when we'd finished. The bottom bed was for the

grown-ups and the top for the children. More often than not my brother and I would take along a friend with us and we would happily sleep with four of us in the top bunk, my brother and I in the middle and our friends on either side of us. Funny how simple life was then. Today it would be considered quite improper for boys and girls of nine to thirteen years of age to be sleeping together, but then it was the norm and without problems.

Rita Game

Sunday Roast

As an adult it never ceases to amaze me that our mum still always cooked meals for all the family after working all day. Even at weekends we had a cooked breakfast and Sunday roast which was the best you could ever taste. This was all cooked on an open fire outside the hut. If it rained, she used the fire in the cookhouse, shared with the other hoppers. Sunday was when all the visitors came down and Mum always managed to feed them as well.

Maureen Vinall

A Pramful of Chickens

Another time I remember very well was when the farmer's chickens went missing and he came round to the hop huts looking for them. My dad hid them in my pram and I was sitting on them so the farmer couldn't see them. We had them for dinner that night.

Pat Frost

The Hewitt family at the bines, c. 1923. The picture was donated by Mr D. Hewitt, who was a social worker with Deaf Welfare in Bromley. Mr Hewitt's brother was deaf, as were the twin girls in the centre of the photograph.

Inside the Hut

The first night was always strange. Oil lamps hung on the wall with moths and other flying insects attracted to the light. The crockery, cups and saucers were kept on the portable dresser suspended from two large coach nails which my mother had knocked into the wall in the early 1900s. Our hut was always number 9. It was brick built with a red-tiled roof. At the rear of the huts, in behind the cooking sheds, were the toilets! These had a long, low, wooden fronted fence, having a top plank which was the seating. The space behind the wooden seating was treated with lime daily. No water flush. Males and females were separated only by a sacking divider across the middle of the wooden seat. To the rear of the cook hut in front of the toilets was a stream running through the adjoining field. It was fed by water from the mill pond which was up the slope from the field about two or three hundred yards away.

L.G. Presley

Hampshire Hops

My family was the only one in the street that didn't migrate to the Kent hop fields in September each year. Our family, together with other members of my extended family living in Stratford and Custom House, were the only people I know who went to Bentley in Hampshire for our annual hop picking holiday. As a child and teenager, my mother had gone with her family to Kent where the hop-picking season was longer and the method of collecting and tallying the hops was slightly different from that in the Hampshire area. In 1947 after the war my mothers and sisters had been invited to join

Barbara Beale (now Frost) and her sister Pat.

a friend who picked on a farm at Bentley and found the conditions far better than those she had suffered when picking in Kent.

Rita Game

Nits

When we came home from hopping we always had fleas in our heads and it meant we had to go to a special clinic to have our hair washed in a special, strong soap before we could go back to school.

Pat Frost

The Pictures and the Pub

At weekends when Dad came down I remember everyone going into town on the bus. While one of the dads escorted all the children to the pictures the adults went to the pub. As you can imagine it was a very noisy bus that returned to the farm and the conductor spent most of the journey trying to collect the fares.

Maureen Vinall

Fascist March

Hopping to us was a lovely holiday. One Saturday before we went down to the hop garden, me being the youngest, one of my sisters took me shopping down Tower Bridge Road. I wondered what all the people were doing there and when we got home and told our Dad about it and asked where Mum was. He said that Sir Oswald Mosley, the Fascist, had been doing a march and that Mum had been arrested with her friend, Mrs Gosby, for trying to pull Mosley into the road. The good old days! I remember the police were always big men in those days. If they caught any young people doing anything wrong they would clip them round their ears and take them round home where they'd get another smack from their parents for misbehaving. Can you imagine anyone doing that now? I cried when Mum was arrested and said I was off to the police station to get her home. Dad said 'Let her stop there. It will do her good.'

Ethel Chandler

It's Great to be Back

When we got to Paddock Wood the farm would send a horse and cart to pick all our boxes and luggage up. But lots of us would walk to the farm as it was great to be back in the countryside. The rest of the day was busy settling into our tin huts, sorting out the boxes. We used to have four huts, one each for my mother and her family, her two sisters and their families and one for Granddad. We would get bundles of soft wood called faggots, which were laid on the concrete floor. This was the base of our bed. And then we would stuff dry straw into an old mattress and put it on top of the faggots. It wasn't very comfortable but at least we were off the ground. We took all our own bedclothes and pillows.

Mrs Peggy Carter

Wood Smoke

My main recollection of returning to the hop huts after a day's picking was of lighting a wood fire for cooking. There was a wonderful smell from wood faggots burning bright while we children sat around it during the evenings. We made toast with slices of bread held on long forks and roasted apples stuck on the ends of long sticks, all the while telling each other stories and talking while the evening shadows grew deeper. Burning logs crackled and gave off showers of sparks as they dropped lower in the fire until only the glowing embers remained. Then we were called to bed, a wash and eventually tumbled onto the large straw-filled bed which rustled at every move. Oil-filled lamps flickered on the wall, their smoke-tinted glass chimneys emitting wisps of smoke, undisturbed by the ever present moths fluttering around the light. Warm contentment; happy sleep.

L. Presley

Collecting Water

I was born in 1943 and went hopping until I was seventeen. My name before I was married was Pat Beale. Our family lived at the Elephant and Castle and we used to go to Reave's Farm about three miles outside of Hadlow. We went into Hadlow for our shopping. The pump where we had to get our water every day was about half a mile away from the hop huts. We took buckets and jugs but we always managed to get more in our shoes before we got back to our hut. Also, we used to use a big stick to carry the buckets and jugs on, with one of us at each end.

Pat Frost

The Pearly King and Queen of Harrow collecting for charity at Rochester, 5 September 1999.

Pearly Kings and Queens

The 'Pearlies', or Pearly Kings and Queens of London, were mostly hop pickers and still attend hop picking festivals at Faversham and Paddock Wood. Brian and Margaret Hemsley are the Pearlies of Harrow. Margaret's mother was a hopper and picked at Old Tudeley and Eridge near Crowborough. The Pearly Queen of Whitechapel, Nanny Armstrong, was also a regular hopper and on returning to their former hop farm recently, discovered their old hut was the only one that had not been demolished.

HH

Mum's Revenge

My mum was the boss in our house. She worked damned hard, while Dad liked his drink. One day before I was born my mum took the children to The Horns public house and said to the barman 'Is Jim Ash in there?' He said yes, so she sent all the children in to him. 'Tell your father to look after you.' The women worked hard and the men drank all the money away. I loved hopping. We had a lovely gipsy who always looked after the kids when it was cold and wet. The farmers made us go out and pick in all weathers but there didn't seem to be the amount of illness around that there is today, even if you did have to keep the fleas and bugs down. If any one of us used to cry with the earache our mothers used to fill the pillows up with hops and it eased the pain.

Ethel Chandler

Falling in the Fire

When Maureen [Vinall] was only five or six she insisted on going with Edie, our sister, who didn't want her tagging along yet again. Maureen ran across the common after Edie, not looking where she was going, fell into the cooking fire and burnt her arm, causing panic all round and a few sorry faces. One year we were all packed to go home but the lorry didn't arrive. There we were – two families, the Jenkins and the Sullivans, stranded overnight with eight kids on one bed of straw.

Michael Jenkins

Determined to Enjoy it

Unlike the children the adults had everyday tasks to perform: cooking, washing clothes, washing up etc., after which they could relax for the evening. We were a community of like-minded city dwellers having a working holiday in the fresh air and although it was not all holiday for the grown-ups and often very hard work, we were determined to enjoy it.

L. Presley

Caught Scrumping

One pastime of us children was to go scrumping. Once when doing this I was caught red-handed in his orchard by the farmer. Filling my pockets with apples, I ran all the way back to the huts whilst being chased. One apple was so big I couldn't remove it before the farmer caught me at the hut. He let me off with a warning to Mum that if I did it again she could be sent home (disaster!). On another occasion I was caught by a farmer with a shotgun – I was terrified! The annual challenge was to get into the Cox's Pippins orchard.

Michael Jenkins

Rabbit Stew

My cousins were quite a bit older than me and some of them were married. They would take it in turns to cook the evening meals. Wild rabbits were caught and skinned then popped into the pot to make delicious stews. I can remember when I was about eight or nine I found various farmland produce such as potatoes, apples and pears, to cook on the

Whitbreads children's party at the end of hop-picking (courtesy of the Hop Farm Country Park).

grid when my aunt's back was turned. I never had much success though and, looking back, I'm sure I was too impatient and expected them to cook in five minutes. I finally gave up when a potato I had forgotten and left on the grid exploded making everyone in the cook house jump and showering the company with bits of red hot potato. Needless to say I got a good ticking off from Aunt Mag. After that I stuck to blackberry picking and my lips, tongue and fingers were permanently stained with purple juice.

Maureen E. White

Preparing to Leave

The fields were cleared of all bines and we started to think of home. We children realised it was the end of the work. Although we were sad to leave friends made during the hop-picking, and while it had been a lot of fun, it had also been hard work. There was the sad task of packing up all our personal belongings into the waiting hopping box which was lifted up onto the back of the lorry for our journey home.

L. Presley

Playing in the Bins

I remember walking down the lane in the dark with just a torch and nearly falling in a ditch. The farmer, Mr Tibbles, emptied boxes of apples on the grass so we kids could pick them up to take home. Sometimes if I pulled down a bine the lot would fall on your head. I had long hair and when I played with the other children I got nits so it was

cut short and Mum had it permed. We had to wait for the tractor to take us if we were working in the top hopfield. Sometimes I was put in the hop bin as a joke then covered over with hops.

Christine O'Connell (née Leach)

The Hopping Routine

My family went hop picking at Wateringbury from 1925 to 1938. We had a regular plan for going and this is what I enjoyed best. 1: Prepare for travel: Make up cart for transport of clothing, bedding, utensils etc. 2: Load up cart less wheel shafts onto the lorry together with other families and their carts. Adults had to push lorry up steep inclines. 3: Arrived at Mill Farm, Wateringbury, and allocated hut (ours was hut 9). Farmer on cart delivered bundles of faggots to use as the base of the bed and for our cooking fires. Made up beds with some branches from faggots. Stuff mattress and pillows with straw from farmer. 4: First day at hop field: collect bin and take it to our allotted lane in the field. 5. Take food and large pots of hot tea. Heavy clothes – weather always cold in the early morning. 6: Set up hopping bin. 7: Pickers picked hops; no leaves or twigs accepted. Our pole puller was Bob Buckley who lived in a cottage near the pickers' huts with his wife Jane and son Tom (nicknamed 'Tommy Sausage'). Bob pulled down the higher bines using a curved-bladed hook on a long, wooden pole. If we had finished picking one bine and needed another we called out 'Pole Puller!' If we needed the Measurer because our bin was getting full we called 'Here Measurer!' The measurer scooped hops from the bins into sacks or pokes while the tallyman recorded the amount we had picked and the Recorder recorded our earnings. 7: Back home to South London at Newington Butts at the Elephant and Castle. 8: End of a wonderful holiday. Mum never scrimped; always provided the best she could afford but her greatest contribution was love. 9: The evening's entertainment was the best; children sat around fires in the cook hut, happily talking while roasting apples on sticks. Adults sometimes went to the public house for a drink and a sing song. 10: 'Last Bines!'

L. Presley

Daily Duties

Each day there would be the same duties. There would be my gran, my mum, brother and myself and all of us would be around our bin, picking off the hops. Each family had their own row and each family would be round their own bin doing the same as us. We came from Dartford, where I went to the National School on West Hill. It is no longer open.

Stan Dalton

Picking Clean

A time-saving tip was to make sure you picked the hops clean; by this I mean you had to make sure you didn't get any leaves in the bin. The farmer made us take them all out before the tally so it was time and money wasting if you had to clean up your hops. He also made sure we picked up any that had fallen on the floor. I remember Mum queuing with her book to get her money and on the way home she would

Michael Whiteside and family at Whitbreads.

ask Mr Grey to stop at the store and she would go in and buy loads of groceries; which was lovely because normally we never had a lot of food at any one time.

Stan Dalton

The Cookhouse

Cooking facilities had moved on by the time I was taken hop-picking. The cooking was still done outside the huts but the farm had provided a cookhouse. This was a three-sided wooden structure with a high roof, the top of which had a wide hole to let out the smoke and steam. This was fine until the wind blew in a certain direction or it rained. The

Kevin Parry, with his parents Nellie and George Parry, at their hop hut at Plumford Farm, Faversham, c. 1959.

cookhouse would fill with smoke and everyone would be coughing and spluttering, eyes streaming and unable to see what they were doing. Each family was allocated a cooking space. This consisted of a square of rough brickwork about nine or twelve inches high with a grid laid on top. Fires were lit first thing in the morning and kettles put on to boil. Once the tea was made, breakfast preparation commenced. The fire would be re-lit when we got back from the fields. Everything cooked was either boiled or fried. Butcher's and grocer's vans came round two or three times a week. They had to toot their horns down by the five-bar gate and the women would carry their baskets across the field to shop. Milk and dairy produce was bought from the farmer.

Maureen E. White

Successful Strike

The third time of going hop-picking I was eighteen and went with a friend and her family. They had been hop-picking for many years to a place called Kingston Bagpuize, Oxon. The huts there were wood and had a ledge along the inside to serve as a bed for my friend and myself. We had a hut to ourselves with plenty of straw to make up a mattress. We had to help with the hop picking. Most of the time you had to walk to the hop fields, but if it was a long way the farmer would take us to the garden on a lorry or tractor. The pickers went on strike for more pay – which we got. There was a pub about a mile from the site where the adults went and a village hall which held dances every Saturday night. There were no lights anywhere as

the war was on and if the lights were on the enemy knew where to drop their bombs. We really enjoyed ourselves. Of a night we used to sit around one another's huts telling stories. We had three weeks picking at Kingston Bagpuize then it was back to London and I had to go on war work, being eighteen. They are good memories.

Mrs A. Hamlin

Black Hands

There was a problem with the state of our hands, which were black from the hop juice. No rubber gloves in those days!

Mrs B. Easdown

Lollies!

We lived in New Road, Rotherhithe. We did have great times. The baker came regularly to the Common, with lovely pies, cakes and bread. The Liptons van brought us groceries to buy and there was the lollipop man with his basket of sweets coming up the hopfield ringing his bell and calling 'Lollies, lollies!' He wore a big cap and plus-four trousers with brightly coloured socks. I think that was in 1937.

Pat and George Cole

Pausing for a pint at Whitbreads in the 1950s (courtesy of the Hop Farm Country Park).

CHAPTER 7

Preparing the Hops

Sampling the hops (courtesy of the Hop Farm Country Park).

Hops need to be picked when they reach their peak. This ensures the brewer will get the best flavour from the resins and essential oils held in tiny capsules at the base of each cone's petal. Nowadays these oils and resins are distilled separately and bottled for use as required. Hops are pelletized in bulk, then freeze-dried in much the same way as coffee granules. This way they can be stored over long periods and used when needed. The hop flower is called by different names according to its growth. From their first appearance to full maturity, these are the hop flower, cone, pin (usually in July),

burr (July, August) and bullet. Hop drying is a skill: too much heat and the hops over dry; too little and they may moulder when packed in the pocket. Either way they cannot release their flavour. Freshly garnered hops are spread out on the upper stage – hessian or horsehair – of the oast house floor. Heat is generated by a ground floor kiln which may be fuelled by charcoal or oil. Once the hops are roasting the fires must not be left unattended. This could mean the kiln man sleeps and eats near the kiln at all times as he has to check the gauges regularly to ensure the temperature remains even. Hops contain 80 to 85 per cent moisture when first picked and this has to be reduced to 6 to 10 per cent, evenly distributed across the load. It takes eight hours at 140° Fahrenheit to dry a kiln load of hops laid out first on a kiln's horse-hair blanket, then on the oast house drying floor. Whitbreads multiple kilns could deal with 20,000 bushels per day. Until it was discontinued in the 1980s, sticks of sulphur were put in a metal pan and added to fire so the fumes they gave off rose to the drying hops. This helped to give a characteristic flavour and appearance to the beer as well as improving their keeping qualities. Sulphur was commonly utilized in a variety of processes up until the 1970s: a stick of sulphur was sometimes burned in a parasite-infested house to cleanse it. A common recipe for children was 'brimstone and treacle' (brimstone being another name for sulphur) to thin their blood after winter so they didn't develop ulcers and abscesses in the summer. Sulphur was used to dust crops to kill off harmful infestations. It was listed as a constituent of gunpowder in my school chemistry book (yes, I did try it out!). Once the hops were roasted they were scuppered onto the drying or cooling floor to be dried for some twelve hours. Workers continually turned the hops, using either the scuppet or blunt-tined hop dog, to ensure even drying. Once the hops were thoroughly dry they were taken to the press to be rammed into a 7ft long cylindrical sack called a pocket. This was originally worked by means of a man standing in the pocket and acting as a human ram, but then the hop press was invented, enabling the job to be done much faster and more efficiently, although it was still hand-operated. Pokes were shorter, narrower sacks used to transport hops from the hop garden to the oast. Once the hops were pocketed, they were kept in cold-store warehouses to be sampled, assessed and stored until needed.

Eventually, most hops were sent to the Hop Exchange in Borough High Street, Southwark, to be auctioned off to the highest bidders representing various breweries. Not all hops went through this procedure, explained Mark Dobner, head brewer of Shepherd Neame, Faversham. They and other breweries usually forward contracted through their agents for the hops they wanted to ensure they got supplies from designated farmers whose crops were grown specifically for them. The use of an agent, rather than dealing directly with hop farms, was in case anything happens to a particular farmer's crop such as an attack of wilt, as this could leave the brewery short.

The Hop Exchange

We lived at the Elephant and Castle and when the hops had been packed into pokes they were sent up to near here at Great Guildford Street. At London Bridge is Borough High Street which is where the Hop Exchange was. It's not used for that now, but over the doorway of the building you can still see an impressive frieze showing hop-pickers, pole pullers and other hop-picking jobs being done. Down in Southall Street near Borough High Street are the old offices of F. & E. May who owned several hop farms at one time. It's no longer owned by May's but the building is still there and so is the frieze. I'm the Pearly King of Bow Bells and the Pearlies do a lot of charity work, raising funds for hospitals, old people's and children's homes. You usually see them with a charity box in their hand, so give them a 'hello' and help to do a bit of good for others when you see them.

Tom Johnson

Drying the hops at Whitbread's in the 1950s (courtesy of the Hop Farm Country Park).

Drying the Hops

When they used to dry the hops, I helped. In the oast house they had a big net, made of sacking; very heavy sacking. You'd go in there with nothing on your feet and you'd shovel the hops over with your feet to turn them. But as you looked down you could see this great big fire! But you couldn't fall through it or anything because it was strong sacking. The blokes who used to dry the hops never had any sleep. They stayed awake all day and all night because you had certain times for the hops to come out so that they weren't dried too much. Then they had to go into big sacks and then a man comes with what they call a presser and then they take a sample away to let you know if the hops are good. Because in them days you had them for beer but now they also use the hops for dyes.

Alice Heskitt

Children's Games

Once they were allowed off the hop-picking, we didn't see the children until dinner-time. Ours would go off into the woods and build dens, climb trees or collect conkers to thread on strings and have conker fights 'to the death'. Once, our youngest didn't come back even when we were ready to start dinner and we began to think he must have had some sort of an accident, so I sent all the others off to look for him in the woods and the men went down by the river, just in case. About an hour later someone found him: He had climbed a hawthorn tree to get back his ball which had stuck up in the branches only he'd got stuck as well. The ball was shaken out of the tree when he started up into the thinner branches and the thorns were that thick they'd wrapped up in his jumper and he couldn't get away from them or even take his jumper off, so he'd stayed there, yelling for help. If we hadn't found him he could have been there all night.

George Green

Farm Horses

The hops which were picked in the morning were taken up to the oast house on three farm wagons, each pulled by pairs of horses. It was the same again in the afternoon, but different horses, because those used at mid-day had to take some pickers (home-dwellers) back home to Faversham. Also, these horses had fetched them in the morning to take them to the hop gardens, so the same horses had started their day at 5 a.m. But after the journey to town and back they went back into their stables for a two or three hours' rest, then it was up to the hop garden for their first journey to the oast Their second journey was with the mid-day taking of hops.

Ted Bingham

Pat Cole's mother, sister Mavis and brother Billy at Goose Green Farm, Hadlow, in 1952.

DATE	BAT No.	NAME	HUT No	BUSHELS at 4/4	TOTAL	RAIL FARE	TOTAL	LESS SUBS	FINAL TOTAL
Sep 29	1	Dench	4	328	21 17 4	18 3	22 15 7		22 15 7
	2	Harvey	9	658	43 17 4	1 16 7	45 13 11	6	39 13 11
	3	Harrison	55	556	37 1 4	1 10 11	38 12 3		38 12 3
	4	Parry	15	393	26 4	10 11	26 14 11		26 14 11
	5	Heard	14	420	26 13 4	11 2	27 4 6	10	17 4 6
	6	Parry (B)	13	284	18 18 8	7 11	19 6 7		19 6 7
	7	Parry (J)	51/32	362	24 2 8	10	24 12 8		24 12 8
	8	Parry (E)	81/32	308	20 10 8	8 6	20 19 2		20 19 2

Part of a page from the Plumford Farm hop ledger, showing Kevin Parry's family registered as pickers in 1955.

Pole Pulling

Dad and I were both pole pullers. Dad had the knack of picking hops very fast by stripping the bine in a certain way and one year he teamed up with Bess who was also a fast picker. He got me to pull the bines for them, so it meant that I did all the work pulling down the bines fast for them but they got the money for picking the hops! We particularly liked to pull down the 'heads' or top of the bines. This was a pole-puller's job as they were too high to reach, otherwise. The heads always had the biggest hops. It took ten bushels of hops to fill one hop pocket. I have family living in Canada and they still love to hear the old hop stories.

Tom Johnson

Hide and Seek

At the bottom of Cut Throat Alley, near the gateway to the field where the hop huts were, was the oast house where hops were dried and bagged into large sacks or pokes. These were stored below on the open–fronted floor of the oast house. As children we played hide and seek here. Beside the oast house was a large horse-chestnut tree so in September we were all well supplied with conkers for our games.

L. Presley

Saturday Night

Saturday night everyone went down to the village. The green and the pub were packed.

It was like being at the fair. Tradesmen from London came down selling everything. Some of the men would go straight to the pub. We wanted to see the shops to make sure they were all still there, then down to the farm. When the pubs kicked out we would all go rolling down the country lanes singing all the old songs till we got to our huts, then we'd sit round the fire in the cookhouse, talking and singing until bedtime.

Jean Pilbeam

Hopping the Wag

At school one of my teachers used to rap you over the back of your neck or across your knuckles with a ruler. My friend and I were always hopping the wag [truanting]. Monday mornings were terrible as that was when the priest came and we were each asked if we'd been to Mass on the previous Sunday. One day I had a row with my friend Nellie; you know what kids are like. Well I didn't go to Mass so I asked Nellie if she had been and because we'd had this argument she was still mad at me and told me the wrong priest, so when the school priest asked me about Sunday Mass I got it all wrong and got into trouble.

Ethel Chandler

Dogs

An unwritten rule in the hop gardens was that all dogs had to be kept under control and not allowed to run about where they liked. Sometimes Hoppers brought dogs down with them and they had to be tied up.

Ted Bingham

Taking in Washing

My mother was the only one down the street who had a wooden wringer so she took in washing at twopence a time. I used to hate Mondays, what with the smell of the washing and the steam and having to turn the handle of the wringer. With all this, we used to look forward to hopping just to get away from it all.

Ethel Chandler

Bin Men

The bin men's job was to help any pickers having difficulty pulling down their bines, also if the head of the bine got stuck on the top wire or had grown up one of the poles he'd use a hook to get it free. This was a pole about 9ft long with a sharp cutting blade and a small spike on it. These were for cutting bine heads down, or maybe for pushing it up and off the top of the pole. The bin men also had to help taking in the hops – some held the pokes open for hops to be put in and then threw the tied up bags onto the waiting wagons which the horsemen held steadily in place. On average, a wagon took between thirty and forty pokes of hops to each load.

Ted Bingham

Evening Meals

The things I remember eating best were fried sausages, mashed potatoes and tomatoes all in thick gravy. Whoever was in the cook house watched over people's pots and pans on their fires. The cook house was

Tallying off at Whitbreads, 1920s (courtesy of the Hop Farm Country Park).

a big tin hut with just a roof, a brick wall down the centre and a big iron bar going from one end to the other. We had hooks on the pots that clipped on the bar and the frying pan would be on the embers of the fire.

Jean Pilbeam

The First Day

The first day's picking was so exciting. We were given our rows of bines to be picked, with our bins. Our mother and her sisters used to work together. All the older children were expected to do quite a lot of picking through the day. The younger ones mostly played and rested. We used to sing and chat while we worked and we all looked forward to having a small treat when the Lolly Man came round with his box of gobstoppers, lollipops and jellied sweets. We took our lunch up the fields and boiled up the billy can on an open fire. Sometimes the butcher's man came round with hot pies for sale. That was a real treat. Once we had finished picking and our hops were all measured out, we went back to the huts then Granddad and the boys lit the outside fire to cook the main meal for the evening. After we'd eaten, the mothers gave the young children a strip wash and put them to bed before we all enjoyed a couple of hours round the fire with hot cocoa and then bed for everyone.

Peggy Carter

Outside Toilet

We didn't get long holidays like they do now so our parents were always in trouble for keeping us away from school too long. Mind you it didn't stop anyone from going hopping! We lived in a very old house; one up and one down. It had a big wash house at the back with a boiler. There was an old fashioned grate in the living room which we had to cook by. The toilet was right down at the bottom of the yard and we had to cut newspaper in squares and thread them onto string to hang up for the toilet.

Ethel Chandler

Animal Mad

My father was animal mad. Every Sunday he went to Petticoat Lane and would come back with all kinds of animals. The neighbours used to call out to my mum 'Ash, see what your old man's bringing home!' We had chickens, rabbits and one Sunday we had a goat. Mum wasn't pleased. Dad shut it up in our front room and it ate my mum's best lace curtains. She was so cross she sent one of my brothers to sell it. We had ducks and they used our big tin bath in the summer. We emptied it once a week so we could all have a bath in it. In the winter we had the tin bath in the wash house. There was a black couple living next door who had two white daughters and the rest were all black. When they moved my dad knocked down the dividing yard wall so we had a bigger yard. He built a wooden hut there and the boys slept in it in the summer. In the end house where Mrs Murphy lived, she was always drunk. One night at midnight she came running out screaming 'The Thames is flooding over!' She was right; we were flooded out.

Ethel Chandler

It Was an Honour

I was entrusted with the tallyman's job in 1957 and 1968. I thought it was an honour to be asked to do it. It was then I found there was a lot of responsibility went with the job. Firstly, I was responsible for the behaviour of all the pickers as well as the work done by all the bin men. Sometimes the work went smoothly through the day without any problems. On other days it was all ups and downs and nothing went right. Wednesdays and Saturdays were very busy days for me because these were the days I had to pay any money to the basket holders who wanted money on account; this was called their subs, or subbing. None was paid during the first seven days of picking because there had to be so many six-bushel tallies booked on their tally card before they could start borrowing. For safety's sake, so everyone knew what was right, they had to sign for any money they subbed in their tally book which I carried, so there could be no arguments later.

Ted Bingham

CHAPTER 8

From Oast to Brewery

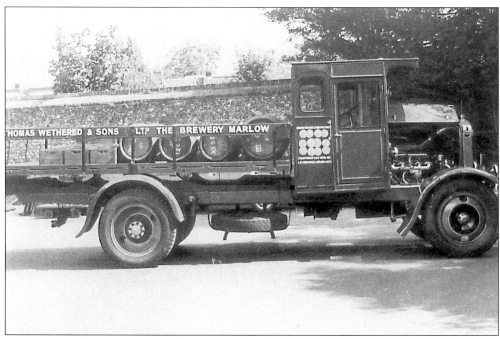

A 1930s brewers' dray (courtesy of the Hop Farm Country Park).

'Hops are valued either for their bittering qualities or aroma, defined by the constituents of their resins and essential oils and it is these virtues that determine the basic brew as ale, beer or lager,' explained Shepherd Neame's Senior Brewer, Mark Dobner. In fact Henry VIII preferred his ale without the taste of hops and actively banned their use in England.

Before the fourteenth century hops were not in common use in beers; those without hops became 'ale' and the hopped variety became 'beer'. By the eighteenth century most beers contained hops. Stout contains a higher quantity of roasted malt. Beer is made from hops, extract of malted barley and is fermented by yeast. The production of one barrel of beer requires one pound of hops, the same of maltose (a barley sugar) one and a half bushels of barley, liquor, a handful of yeast, another bushel of hops plus a commercial sugar to aid fermentation. Yeast is not an ingredient of beer; it is necessary to the fermentation process but is removed after this stage of the operation. This is a simplified version of the brewing process: first, an infusion is made by milling barley malt, called grist, with brewing liquor. The sweet wort separated off from the grains is boiled up with the hops and sugar. Sugar is optional. Towards the end of the boiling an extra addition of hops is made; the amount depends on whether the brew is to be ale, beer or lager. Strong ales need up to 4lb of hops per barrel but delicately flavoured beers may only need 1lb. When the wort has cooled and yeast has been added, the resulting liquor is allowed to ferment. During fermentation, the 'head' of yeast can expand up to 4ft high. Once the senior brewer is satisfied the process is complete, the beer is run into tanks to clarify, and is then bottled or casked. Nowadays hops can be pelletized in a similar process to freeze-drying coffee, using nitrogen. The pellets, known as hoplets, look similar to rabbit food and will keep for up to four years if vacuum-packed and kept in cold store. In this way a 75kg pocket of freshly dried hops can be reduced to two 25kg boxes of pellets.

Sunday Routine

Unlike today, horses and carts did most of the carrying of hops to the oast house and also much of the general work on the farm. Every Sunday afternoon we had a Church Representative visit us on the meadow, leading us in singing hymns and Bible reading. After lunch, if the weather was fine, we walked into town to enjoy our leisure time in the park, or went to the cinema if it was raining. At night, after a day in the hopfields during the week, we sat around the fire talking, playing guessing games and having a sing-song. On Sunday mornings we had a huge fry-up breakfast outside on trestle tables then I used to go for a walk with a friend or my brother to collect elderberries so that our nan could cook them with apples and make an elderberry and apple suet pudding in a cloth.

Joyce Ashby

Pecks and Bushels

During the day the bins would be emptied by an employee of the owner who called out how many pecks or bushels the bin held; as the tally man was usually some way behind calls of 'six!' 'eight!' or 'nine!' usually became seven, nine or ten etc. – this was a sort of perk for the pickers.

Jim Wood

Lodging the Pickers

I used to put some of the Londoners up in my own house. They'd sleep on the floor and everything! First, I started with just a couple of them. I said 'Oh, save you going in the hop huts' because they used to have straw mattresses in the huts you know, straw pillows and that. We had a big copper in the kitchen to boil the water in. My husband would get the cold water from the well and I'd fill the copper. We used to have a long bath by the fire and all of our Londoners used to take turns to bath by the fire in that. We had to keep filling the copper and emptying this great tin bath, but it was great fun really.

Alice Heskett

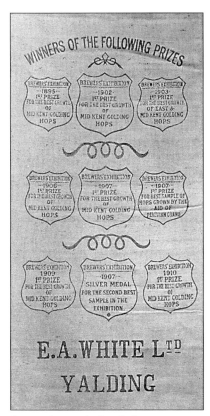

A hop pocket marked with the owner's name and awards.

Pockets of Hops

The hops were put into large sacks, lifted onto a horse-drawn cart and taken to the oast house to be dried. Then they were put into long white bags called pockets, then onto the backs of lorries to be taken up to the brewery.

Jean Pilbeam

The End of Hand Picking

The oast had four kilns which could dry sixty twelve-bushel bags of hops at each session of twelve hours. So this shows that the maximum number of bags the oast could take twice daily was 240 twelve-bushel bags of hops. Sadly no hand picking is done now. It's all machinery picking. The family of farmers I worked for use four machines now and they make up for all the hand pickers we used in the old days for the same job. I retired in 1977 so I don't know when they finally stopped all the hand pickers coming to the farm. I think I'm right in saying that the first mechanical picking machine was installed for the 1957 season. This was when the number of three tallies was cut down to only one tally. Some pickers still had to be employed because about twenty-two men were needed for driving the tractors and some were necessary to do the work in the hop garden, cutting down bines and loading them onto the trailers to take to the machine. Five more were needed as bin men. Also, I have no idea when the call to work was stopped, or the call to stop picking that lasted from twelve to one o'clock.

Ted Bingham

Playing Around

In the hop fields when you had a lot of hops in the bin sometimes other hoppers would come up behind you and dump you in the bin. They did this to my mum a few times and fooled around trying to put hops in her mouth and maybe close the bin. She took it all in good part but on one of these occasions I had my hand on the wooden edge of the bin and when it was closed my fingers got squashed and I had to be taken to the farmhouse where they put iodine on them. It really stung.

Mrs Joan Lewer

The Law

When they've been picked the hops are taken to the oast house to be dried. It was a specialist job really, and a man had to know what he was doing to be allowed onto the drying floor, so it was usually done by locals, but sometimes men who had been down the hop farm regularly each year were allowed to do the job. It takes about nine or ten hours just to dry one batch of hops, so it's a long process to get through a whole crop. Then they have to be cooled, then they're packed very tightly into pockets using a hop press. A pocket weighs about 1½cwt then someone would come along with a stencil and ink and mark every pocket with the date and the grower's name or farm name, and the parish it came from. This was by law, so farmers couldn't pull a fast one and slip some

of last year's crop into this year's batch of pokes. In the old times it got so serious (some farmers who'd had a poor yield in a year felt they could make up for it by cheating a bit by slipping in a few extra pokes left over from before), that the Government put two Acts through Parliament, one in 1774 and the second in 1866 (after some farmers found ways to get around the first Act). These forced farmers to label their pockets with letters at least three inches high. Some of the more canny farmers thought that if they started numbering their pockets much higher at 2,000 or 3,000 rather than just from number one it would fool other growers into thinking the yield was very high that year and they'd not expect to get a such high price for their crop. Hops were commercially classed as 'East Kents', 'Bastard East Kents',

Hop pellets, a hop sample from
Neckington Farm and a spray of
fresh hops.

'Mid-Kents' and 'Wealds' to show roughly where they were grown. This was because they grew on different kinds of soil. East Kents were grown mainly on chalklands, Mid-Kents were from the London Tertiaries, Wealds came from Weald clay districts around Tunbridge Wells and the Hastings area and Bastard Kents grew between East Kent and the Weald. East Kents have always produced the highest quality of crops and, generally, the Wealds gave a slightly lower calibre.

George Green

Bad Weather Days

If the weather was bad there was no picking. It was lovely not having to work so we'd go scrumping, tying string round the bottoms of our trousers and slipping apples down the legs. Sometimes we had so many we could hardly walk. If the farmer caught us there would be the devil to pay and sometimes he wouldn't let you come down to pick the next year. How many weeks we were picking depended very much on the weather but it was normally all in September. If our fields were finished the farmer would ask if anyone wanted to work on and help another farmer to pick his hops and he would take us to the other farmer's field each day.

Jean Pilbeam

A-Frames and Alleys

Each family of hop-pickers were allocated an alley along which they worked, picking hops from the cut-down bines and into the bin. The bin was composed of two long,

horizontal shafts mounted each side of two A-frames located about two feet from each end. The tops of the A-frames formed carrying handles so we could move the bin along. It looked like a litter or stretcher because between the A-frames and the wooden shafts was attached a large piece of hessian sacking hung to form a bag or trough for collecting our hops as we picked them. The A-frames were made to open out at the bottom when resting on the ground. When we had finished picking in one alley, the hop bin had to be picked up and the sides pulled close so it wasn't so difficult to carry it to the next drift, then it was stood in place ready to start picking the next alleyway until they had all been picked clean.

L. Presley

Dirty Picking

I had one nasty incident during my spell as a tally man. This was because of a Scotsman who lived on one of the encampments. He would not pick the hops clean (he kept adding in bits of branches and leaves, known as a dirty picker). There would be four or six complete branches in each of his baskets of hops. I had to tell him that if he did not stop doing this he would be shot onto the job of cleaning the leaves and branches out of everyone else's hop baskets. He had to be given two such warnings before this would be done. He threatened me with violence, which I did not want, so I informed the Head Office of the situation. The next time I was taking the measure, two men stood close by to his row in the garden watching what happened. Unfortunately he had made no effort at all to pick his hops without branches and leaves so I had no

Peggy Carter's dad helping with the pokes, 1949.

option but to lay some bags on the ground ready for him to clean up his hops. He realised what I was about to do and angrily reached out to strike me, but before he could touch me he was restrained by two bin men who grabbed him and told him not to be so silly. But by then the two men sent from Head Office who had been watching what was going on, came forward and told him who they were. One was a police officer in civilian clothes and he gave the man a lecture and a warning about his future behaviour. The second man was the company's head clerk, who added up the man's total of tallies and odd bushels which had been written in his tally card by me, and was in the tally book which I carried with me and entered all the pickers' tallies, then they paid him so much a bushel and gave him notice to be off the farm by mid-day the following day and to never come back to the garden.

Ted Bingham

The Pie Man

About ten o'clock someone would light a small fire and our mum made a pot of tea. Vans came to the fields selling bread, pies, cakes and ice cream (if your mum could afford it). At dinner time the fire was lit again but you would be further down the row by then. We would have a mug of tea with our sandwiches, eaten with our fingers

Three horse-brasses. The top one shows hop pickers at Faversham, and is available from the Fleur de Lys Heritage Centre, Faversham.

one month they were cut off about six inches from the ground and if they were not wanted for anything they would be burnt. After this, the farmyard manure was spread for the hops and then the ploughing was done to put the manure in the ground. First one pair of horses was used to pull a baulker up the centre of each alley. This implement made a V shape in the ground that was about 8 inches deep. Then another pair of horses pulling a plough would follow, ploughing one furrow from the left-hand side back into the baulk furrow before coming back on the right hand side and filling the baulk furrow up. Then a third pair of horses followed on, only this time the plough would take another furrow off and leave about a 12-inch-wide piece of soil along each side of the hills. But where the alleys were 8ft wide, three furrows had to be taken off each side of the baulk. After this the workmen had their bit to do. They dug the remaining soil away from the hills, turning it into the furrow as they went along each aisle. Their pay for doing this work was according to the number of hills and they got paid by the hundred. It was hard work and each man doing it worked cant by cant. There were so many rows to a cant and some were twelve, others were eight; it all depended on how many hills there were to a row.

Ted Bingham

all green or black from picking the hops. At the end of the day someone would shout 'Pull no more bines!' and that was to tell us we had to finish the bine we were working on and then we could go back to the huts.

Joan Lewer

After the Picking

Until the 1970s the hop gardens were cultivated after the hops had been picked. The bine was left hanging on the breast wire or lying on the ground to dry. After about

The Privy

Machine picking arrived at Plumford Farm in the early 1960s but the farmer still kept on hand pickers. The machine shed was built opposite our huts. Although the huts were demolished many years ago some structures still remain there, including a double toilet hut. This was a hut with a long plank of wood, used as a seat and with two holes in it, each sited over the pit. During the picking season the farm hand who drove the horse and cart would bring round quick lime and shovel it down the back of the hut under a flap once a day. It was not very nice if you happened to be sitting there at the time. Come to think of it, the old boy never smiled, but then he did have some horrible jobs. Our water came from stand pipes sited between the rows of huts. We collected our water supply in large enamel buckets with wire handles and a wooden grip.

Kevin Parry

A Quick Wash

After a long day in the fields we were usually pretty tired and were in bed early. We had to fetch all our water from a standpipe so we washed in an enamel bowl at the end of the day, then I would climb into bed while my aunt made a hot drink and then for supper we would have bread spread with condensed milk.

Shirley Thorn

Fun and Games

The last day of picking always brought a lot of fun. People were put in sacks and carried to the oast house, flour bags were thrown freely and people, mainly the adults, all dressed up in fancy dress. The children were just glad they didn't have to pick any more hops.

Joyce Ashby

Locked in the Toilet

At one end of the common there was a row of wooden toilets. One lady walked with a limp and we were told she had a wooden leg. When her friends or relatives saw her go to the toilet they locked her in and rocked the hut backwards and forwards and you could hear her inside, screaming and laughing.

Joan Lewer

Starting New Bines

After the workmen had completed digging the extra soil away from the hills they went back to cut the hop hills in the cants they'd just dug. By this I mean after the bines are cut off there is a small piece left, also a piece like a person's finger growing from the crown of the hill. This had to be cut off leaving the crown of the hill like an upturned basin. These cuttings from the hop hills were used for getting new, young hop sets started growing. The part which was in the ground and about an inch of bine were inserted into the soil, sometimes by the workmen making a slit trench with a spade. This would be done in a spare piece of ground which wasn't being wanted for anything that year. Hops are perennial plants and keep on producing new bines for several years.

Ted Bingham

CHAPTER 9

'A Pint of Your Best'

Saturday night at the pub. Those pictured include: Mr Jim Beale, Mrs Christina Beale, their daughters Chris, Barbara and Pat, Uncle Bob Jukes, the Beales' grandchildren and Ernie.

Taxes of any kind are never popular, and by the eighteenth century the tax on malt was so high it led to an emphasis in the selling of beer rather than ale. Up until the early 1730s the most popular drinks were ale, beer and 'tuppenny': all malt liquors. Tuppenny (two pennies) was a pale kind of small beer: in the grounds of Canterbury cathedral a gravestone is dedicated to a grenadier who died, it claims, from drinking 'small beer'. Sometimes

tuppenny was mixed with ale, called 'half and half'. Equal quantities of tuppenny, ale and beer was called a 'three threads'; this became known as 'porter' and sold at around 3½d for a quart.

Tax on glass was sufficient to prevent beers being sold in bottles. Until the late nineteenth century anyone wanting to take beer home took along his own jug for the purpose. Only when the Government obligingly lowered the glass tax did breweries start selling their beers in bottles, which quickly became popular. Early bottling was hand corked and only from 1908 were the familiar 'crown' metal tops used.

Beer was considered a necessity of life and in the early eighteenth century home brewing was permitted without licence: this is still the case. At that time tea was too costly for the average householder's pocket. The main alternatives for both adults and children's drinks were ale, cider, home-made lemonade for those who could afford the lemons or Adam's Ale (plain water). There were no bottled or cartoned soft drinks.

It is interesting that, while there is a minimum strength allowed for beers, there is no upper limit. Eighteenth-century strong beer was taxed at 2s a barrel while the tax on a barrel of small beer was 6d.

During the Second World War the production of beer increased by some 28 per cent due to the Government supplying beer as essential provisions to the three Services. Breweries co-operated to arrange regular deliveries to garrisons at home and overseas for servicemen as this was considered an important and indispensable morale booster to men fighting away from home.

Whitbreads had some 400 acres under hops by the 1950s. In addition to regular farm workers employed during the first eight months of the year in bine cultivation, five thousand men, women and children were engaged, mostly from London, for the September picking season at Beltring, Paddock Wood.

A 'Decoction of Hops together with Centaury and Camomile' makes a good tonic, I was told by the late Nell Hearson, who also gave me this recipe for parsnip wine:

Take 4lb of parsnips, well washed and cut into small slices. Boil in one gallon of water until tender, then strain. Add to the juice $3\frac{1}{2}$ lb sugar, 1oz dried hop flowers and a generous ounce of crushed ginger root. Boil for five minutes. Turn the liquid into a fermenting crock or jar and while it is still hot, add the rind and juice of one large lemon and $\frac{1}{2}$ lb of unseeded raisins. Spread 1oz of fresh yeast on a slice of toast and add this and $\frac{1}{2}$ lb best wheat to the mixture once it has cooled. Ferment for 14 days then skim and bottle in sterilized bottles. Keep for 9 months to a year before using.

Saturday Evening

On Saturday evenings everyone got spruced up ready to go to the Blacksmith's Arms in Cowden. We walked through the country lanes to the public house; we children explored the hedgerows on the way. I was brought up in Chislehurst from the age of two and there were still open fields and farmland here at the time, yet it was an age of discovery and wonderment for me, as I was sure it must have been for the kids from the East End of London. As children were not allowed in the pubs we sat and played outside, sticking close to the door as we knew that at intervals lemonade and crisps would be sent out for us. Through the open windows we could hear the grown-ups singing. They would start off with songs such as 'Swanee', 'Me and My Girl', and 'Anything Goes', then, as the evening wore on the mood would change and the songs became more sentimental until finally, as the pub turned out, we heard them singing with gusto 'We'll Meet Again' and 'Show me the Way to go Home'.

Maureen E. White

The Kendall family, including George, Mary, John and Nellie.

The Plough Inn

An extract from a historical note on the inn: 'The Plough was built in 1483 when Richard III was on the throne. It was originally two farm dwellings owned by Geoffrey Randelle. In 1804 Thomas Spur sold them to John Tapner Esq., who was granted an ale licence and permitted to sell ales and ciders as a farmer and common beer seller and the property was deemed to be a beer house. In 1880 the executors of the Spur estate sold it to one Thomas Leney, brewer of Wateringbury. At the some time the property became know as the Plough. The reason for this may have been linked with the property's earlier title of 'Mouldboard', as a mouldboard was a part of a medieval plough. In 1951 the house was granted a full licence and today the two old cottages form the Plough Inn.'

The pub was conveniently positioned in Trottiscliffe village, across the road from the Oast House when it still had a hop garden. The bar and restaurant of the Plough Inn are annually decorated with fresh hop bines.

Peter and Denise Humphrey

High Old Times

In all the time we went to Plumford I can't remember any trouble, but we did have some high old times. I remember one year, probably 1961, when the farmer must have done particularly well with his hops, because after the crop was gathered in he arranged a musical evening at the farm and treated us all to fish and chips for supper. It was a right old knees-up.

Kevin Parry

Mill Farm

The geography of Mill Farm remains clear in my mind. Access to the farm was made via a lane from the main road which came through Wateringbury and Mereworth. This was known to us as Cut Throat Alley but is now sign-posted Love Lane. The Mill Pond close by was reached by walking up a slope between two farm buildings. To the left of these was the road or track to the hop fields. It passed a very large building known as the Mayor's House, which always had a mass of yellow flowers growing in its front garden. Along this track was a small public house, the Arrow, which was convenient enough for hoppers to call in for a mid-day drink if required. The pub no longer exists, as the building has now been converted into a private dwelling called the Arrow House in memory of the pub.

L. Presley

A Square Baby

After the day's picking, families went to drink in Goudhurst in the evenings. They had to walk two miles there and back. When they got back to the huts they'd sit around the camp fire telling stories. Sometimes there would be tales of ghosts and someone was sure to go off, dress themselves up in a sheet and come back to 'haunt' us round the fire. We drank at the Eight Bells and the landlord had trouble with some hoppers who'd pinch his glasses, pots (pottery jugs) and strong wooden crates which were handy back at the huts for using as stools round the camp fire. The village policeman took to standing along the road leading to the farm to catch people, and he'd take back the crates or anything else they had pinched as they walked past him. There was a right Cockney lady there called Bess. She could hold her own with the best of them and wouldn't give in to anybody. One night she decided she wanted her own crate to take back to her hut. One of the other hoppers warned her the policeman was only a few yards further up the road and advised her, 'Get rid of the crate!' 'Not after carryin' it all this way I won't!' she said and pushed it up the front of her coat, fastening the buttons over it. When she came to the policeman she walked up to him with her square-looking 'baby' and as calm as you like, asked him 'Excuse me Constable, but can you tell me where is the nearest maternity hospital?' Bess was sixty if she was a day, but the policeman, who knew her for the character she was, just grinned and let her pass on by.

Tom Johnson

No Traffic

Happier times were at the weekends when the families came down and they would all go up to the village green to the pub. When the landlord turned us all out at the end of the evening everyone walked back down the lanes to the hop farm, singing all the old songs. There wasn't any fear of getting knocked down by a car in those days.

Mr T. Ovenell

Pat Frost's mum and dad outside the Harrow pub near Hadlow.

Pretend Cigarettes

We went to The Green every Sunday to the pub and Dad brought us out arrowroot biscuits and lemonade to where we sat outside while they were in having a pint. We used to sneak behind the huts with bits of newspaper and a box of matches, then we'd roll the newspaper up into pretend cigarettes and smoke them. One day the lady in the next hut caught us and said 'If you keep doing that you'll catch yellow pyjamas!' She meant yellow jaundice.

Pauline Hart (née Newman)

Camping in the Huts

We were about thirteen years old when me and my mate Teddy used to cycle down from Old Kent Road to the Kent hopping villages – Goudhurst, Yalding, Beltring and Horsmonden before hop picking was due to start. We'd break into the empty hop huts and camp there for a few days just for somewhere to sleep. When the picking started we went down with our mums and in the evening while they were off to the pub, we went off exploring. It was a sort of holiday for me.

Ron Dunt

Sub Day

Friday was sub day for the weekend shopping, which had to be enough for our dad too for when he came down at the weekends for a drink. He'd bring his friends down and after an evening at the pub they would all sleep on The Green, blotto. Swigs Hole was down a steep hill and somehow they always managed to roll down the hill without once breaking a bottle.

Jean Pilbeam

Weekends

We worked in the garden Saturday mornings up to twelve o'clock, then back to the huts we went for lunch. After lunch the mums washed and changed their dresses then walked to the local shops for food while the granddads and older children looked after the small ones and did chores such as cleaning up the cooking fire. Everyone worked really hard in those days. Sundays were rest days and we always had a church service at the huts by the Salvation Army. They always had treats for the children and willingly gave useful advice to the mothers. They were very kind and helpful. Also Sundays were the days the dads came down from London with a bag of goodies and a little money for the mothers (that is if they had managed to find any work that week if they were working on the docks). They used to take the mums for a drink before lunch and Granddad would stay behind, left in charge of the pot roast on the open fire, cooking for dinner time.

Mrs L.I. Carter

The Plough, formerly the Mouldboard, at Trottiscliffe.

Harvest Supper in Whitbreads Bell 5 Oast, October 1956 (courtesy of the Hop Farm Country Park).

Goudhurst Pubs

In the evenings we might stroll down to the High Street at Goudhurst for a drink in one of the three pubs there: The Vine, The Five Bells were two of them, but that was mostly on Saturday nights when we didn't have to go to work the next day.

Doris Turner (née French)

A Flying Angel

Singing on the way home from the pub continued as we wended our way down the lanes. Being the smallest, one of my cousins, but more often than not my Uncle Jack, would lift me up onto their shoulders and give me a Flying Angel. It was from this vantage point that I caught sight of my first fireflies. I really thought they were fairies and when I said so there were peals of laughter from everyone. I was disappointed to be told they were only insects.

Maureen E. White

Wartime

At the time of the war Whitbreads Farm was one of the most up-to-date hop farms. My mother went to Whitbreads before I was born (she died in 1930 when I was three and a half.) My grandmother brought me and my sisters up and took over the family hut at the farm. From then on we went hop-picking every year. When the war came Nan left me at home in Poplar with my older sister Annie (or Nance, as she was called) to take care of my father who worked on the docks. On the first Sunday that the Germans bombed London, in which three bombs were dropped in our road alone, one demolishing a house only two doors away from ours, Dad told us to get down to Bell Common, Paddock Wood, in Kent, for safety, which we did, of course. When we got out of the train down at Paddock Wood there were planes overhead and their bullets were flying past us so we jumped in a ditch and I remember crying because I wanted to go home. When we arrived at Nan's hut she was shocked to see us as she hadn't expected us.

Louisa Barrington (née *Kettles*)

Remembering the Old Times

I was about seven years old when we started going to a small farm in Horsmonden called Swig's Hole. There were always some empty huts after a few days where people had gone home because they couldn't take to the way of living, which was rather rough. So if friends wanted to come down at the weekends the farmer was good in letting them make use of the huts to stay in. During the week our hut was occupied by my mother, two brothers and myself. My Dad and my sister were working in the week but came down every weekend. Even close neighbours came down. I loved those times. Everybody got dressed up on the Saturday night, even the children, then it was down to the village green where the grown-ups had their tipple and we children drank lemonade. That was the only time we were allowed to stay up late. Alas, it all came to an end when the machines began to take over. I've lived in Wales for the past thirty years and my family are now scattered around Kent. Each year I visit my sister and we go down to Swig's Hole. Sadly, where our huts were it is just grazing land now, but the old cookhouse that we used if it rained, and the old water standpipe are still there and are the only things we could relate to the old times. The farmhouse is exactly the way it was then. We spoke to the farmer who now owns it and explained why we were looking around. He was very understanding and helpful and told us that the farmer who had owned it when we were there is still going strong at the age of ninety-three. Also his son owns another farm in the same area. The farmer allowed us to look round and my sister and I must have looked an odd couple, standing in the middle of an empty field, reliving our old times there. It was wonderful.

Pauline Ansell

Stinging Nettles

Another night on the way home from the pub with the adults I was busting to go to the loo; I was sent behind a hedge. All was well until I squatted down and then I yelped. In the pitch black I had sat in a patch of stinging nettles! My Aunt Mag came scrabbling round the hedge, torch in hand. She knew what had happened and searched around until she found some dock leaves to rub on my skin. I was more cautious after that and, happily, it was an experience I never repeated.

Maureen E. White

With a mixture of fear and curiosity, these children look up for enemy aircraft from a trench during a Second World War air raid (courtesy of the Hop Farm Country Park).

The Start of the War

One of the Sundays we had off the hop-picking turned out to be a nightmare for me. It was 3 September 1939 (the day war broke out) and I was ten years old and didn't know anything about wars. We had been issued these awful gas masks up in London just a few months previously. Most of them were the ordinary black face mask kind but my three-year-old brother Benny and his cousin had Mickey Mouse face masks which were really frightening, especially to Benny. My baby cousin, Margaret, had a cylinder gas cot that we

had to put her into and then zipped it up and pumped the air into it. That was also scary. All of a sudden this awful noise like wailing spread all over the farm and out of the sky came planes diving down at us and ducking and the word spread round the hop field that war was declared and to us older children that meant gas masks! So my cousins and I got all the masks out of their boxes which we'd brought down with us in the hopping box and we got them onto the children, including the Mickey Mouse ones and baby Margaret was put into her cylinder. We told all the children to get into the ditch which ran across the back of the hop huts where we threw all our waste water; so it wasn't a very nice place to be, but it seemed to be a good, safe place at the time. But it was very hard because we had all these distressed children to deal with. My dad and uncle rushed back to the huts from the village pub and found us all in the ditch in a very unhappy state, with the little ones scared and crying. Meanwhile Granddad was still watching the pot roast for lunch and moaning away about the war. We stayed on picking the hops right up till the end of September but everyone was alert to what was happening in the sky all the time we were picking, after that. We never went back to Mayes Farm again, owing to the war.

Mrs L.I. Carter

Drunk at the Camp Fire

In 1957 me and my mate Eddy Woodrow thought we would take a ride to Tonbridge. Eddy had always gone hopping. We were both eighteen at the time and had been waiting two years for the Army call-up and the papers had just come. We called in the pubs and soon started to enjoy ourselves and ended up getting drunk. We walked and walked and came to a common where all the hop-pickers were and they made us very welcome. We fell asleep by their camp fire. When we woke up we didn't know where we were, and to this day we never did find out.

George Taylor

'They've Got Me!'

My mum and dad, Mr and Mrs Beale, went to a farm called Leavers Farm in Hadlow, Kent. They had five daughters and we all went hop-picking. They were Pat, Shirley, Joan and Chris Beale. Mum had to go home to work in between picking, and we had to keep the bin for her for when she came back to the farm. On Sunday lunchtimes we used to go to a pub called the Harrow for a drink. Our aunt was Mrs Kathleen Jukes and she used to take her children hop-picking as well. Hop-picking was very hard work but we all got on with what we had to do and still managed to have a good time, especially us children as it was so nice to be able to get out of town. I particularly remember one funny thing that happened when the war was on. My gran, Mrs E. Beale, was sitting at the bin when a plane came over. We all got down

Damaged bells at Whitbread's after a severe storm (courtesy of the Hop Farm Country Park).

Tom, Karen and Lorraine Wright.

and has hardly changed. On Saturday afternoons we were given a shilling by our parents and we all walked into Faversham to spend it, usually in Woolworths. Sometimes we would walk along Water Lane into Ospringe, which at that time had a stream running down by the road. This disappeared forever when the M2 was built.

Kevin Parry

but my gran was wearing a long black skirt and caught the heel of her shoe in the hem. She didn't realise what was the matter and thought she must have been shot because she couldn't move and kept crying out loud 'They've got me!' We were all laughing. She did see the funny side of it, later.

Mrs B. Kendall

Gone Forever

Our family loved their beer and our favourite and most visited pub was the Alma at Painters Forstal. It is still a very good pub

CHAPTER 10

Pot Pourri

The Parry family (all ex-hoppers) return to Plumford Farm to reminisce. The hop huts used to be on three terraces facing the hop fields.

What do ex-hoppers talk about when they get together? They remember the highlights of each hop-picking holiday, the challenge of making do with what they had. How grateful they were for something as small as a pound of apples or a few eggs. They contrast their days of happy poverty with today's affluent society and the life they lived comes out as tops for happiness. Ex-hoppers are keen to offer reasons as to what must have happened to change society so drastically from responsible, law-abiding citizens to communities where folk are no longer safe in their own homes. They call attention to what they see as a stark contrast between the old ways of what would now be called 'care in the community' and present-day elderly people living behind bolted and barred doors, sometimes even afraid to speak to the folk next door and where someone living alone could be dead a month before anyone knows about it. 'It could never have happened in the old days,' they assert. Where is the close camaraderie once enjoyed by so many? Why are folk always trying to outdo others and are never satisfied with what they already have? Having survived the stringency of wartime Britain, ex-hoppers are scathing of the modern demand for more of everything. Today's people have so much yet want still more. Before the 1950s hardly anyone owned a refrigerator. Televisions had hardly been heard of, most people rented their homes, a family owning a house telephone or car was considered well-off, even posh. There was no such thing as wall-to-wall carpeting; floors had bare boards, sometimes covered in linoleum and with maybe a home-made rag rug in front of the fireplace which burned wood (or whatever could be scrounged) to keep the place warm. There was no central heating and cooking was done on a huge kitchen range that might, if you were lucky, be powered by gas, as were the street lights. Many homes were still lit by gas or paraffin lamps and all food was bought from the corner shop, the Maypole or Liptons. Money was so scarce that Sunday dinner would often only be a scrag end of mutton from the butcher, boiled up with carrots and potatoes and dipped with slices of bread. The only take-away food was fish and chips and pie and mash. Children scrounged discarded vegetables from where they lay on the market road, eager to help swell the family larder. Most loos were outside in a row of terraced toilets or down steps out in the garden: their wooden doors had gaps at top and bottom to let the light in and torn sheets of newspaper were threaded on string and hung on a nail, ready to wipe when necessary. They were freezing in the winter! Coal was kept in the cellar and carried up a steep flight of stone steps when needed. Yet somehow, among all this dire poverty, people accepted their lot, made a point of not complaining, helped their neighbour through any crises and shared what little they

had in a true spirit of generosity. It's not that ex-hoppers feel we should return to the penury or hardships of those days, but they do feel that the advantages of progress are overshadowed by the many disadvantages brought in their wake. Police kept a high profile, walking the streets on regular beats; but there was a real divide between those scrounging coal to keep their home fires burning and the real criminals of the day. Even criminals respected the police. Few carried guns – the additional penalty was too high. Knives were only used by foreigners. Robberies seldom involved vandalism for its own sake and burglars rarely attacked their victims unless challenged. Rape was a hanging offence. By the 1950s the government of the day decided on clearing slum areas and putting tenants into bright new housing. The idea was welcomed by most, especially around city areas where rubble and bomb-damaged houses predominated. People were assured that when they were re-accommodated in council flats they would be moved estate by estate, ensuring continuation among communities and allowing neighbours to live near their friends. Unfortunately this didn't happen. Instead of moving a whole street into one block of flats, bureaucracy channelled officials into allocating accommodation according to council lists. Families were moved arbitrarily, in most cases next to complete strangers. The new, modern accommodation was welcomed but the gain in amenities was at the expense of community spirit. Tenants missed former friends and neighbours on whom they relied. No longer could children pop into Next Door if Mum wasn't home. They, too, lost friends whom they now only saw at school. Keys were no longer left dangling inside letter boxes on bits of string. There was no-one to mind the baby while you popped down to the shops. Granny, cared for by near family and neighbours once her children had moved on, was now entirely alone, stuck in a brand new but empty flat. Where once she could sit out in the street on her chair chatting to friendly neighbours, now she sat in her modern kitchen with not even passers-by to talk to because no-one even knew who she was. It was one thing telling off friends' children who misbehaved; another thing entirely when strangers' children resented what they saw as an outsider's interference. This is why there is a lack of community among modern estate residents who no longer enjoy the benefits of well-established relationships and now live among people they do not know. To begin with, everyone still met up to go hop-picking: one of the last community activities which helped folk keep contact with old mates, but by the early 1960s even that had gone.

Feeding the Hoppers

At the end of hop-picking we always had a cooked dinner for the pickers before they went home. I used to make a meat pudding, potatoes and cabbage and have a sweet at the end. The hop-pickers always had a sing-song and then my husband took them back to Tonbridge station with their bits of luggage and everything at the end of the hop-picking time. It was all quiet and peace. It was terrible! I missed them, I really did. But I always used to say to the Londoners, 'It's all right you coming down to pick – you want to come and train them [the hops]. You wouldn't want the job so quick then!' because it was really hard work, training hops.

Alice Heskitt

Alice remembers the hard work of those days, yet still believes people were happier then. She wrote the following poem:

'Poor but Blessed in the Good Old Days'

We met and married a long time ago.
We worked the hop farm when wages were
low.
No TV, no wireless, no baths. Times were
hard;
Just a cold water tap and a walk to the yard.
No holiday abroad, no carpets on floors.
We had coal on our fires and didn't lock
doors.
Our children arrived: no pill in those days.
We brought them all up – without state aid!
They were safe out to play in the hopfields
or park
And our old folk could safely go out in the
dark.
No valium, no drugs, no LSD.
We cured all our ills with a good cup of tea!
Milkmen and bakers' boys would whistle
and sing.
A night at the pictures was our weekly fling.
We all got our share of trouble and strife:
We just had to accept it; the pattern of life.
Now I'm alone I look back through the
years,
Forgetting the bad times; the trouble, the
tears.
I remember with blessings, our home and
our love,
That we shared them together I thank God
above.

Alice Heskitt

Doodlebugs over Kent

My dad went into the Army like a lot of the men and meanwhile the London raids got worse. Mum decided we ought to be evacuated so we went over to Wales for nearly two years and lived on a farm while

Pat Cole's mum, aunt Queenie, cousin Sally, and Pat herself at Goose Green Farm in 1957.

we were there. Soon after we came back to London the doodlebugs started, which was really scary, and of course Mum worried that we would be bombed. Then she heard from a distant aunt and uncle who lived and worked on Chambers Farm at Sutton Valence in Kent. Apparently the farmer needed people to pick fruit and then hops through the year. This time we had a lovely brick hut which made a real difference to our lives and comfort. It was warm and cosy and there was a Primus stove to cook on. Wonderful! Joyce and Benny, my younger brother and sister, went to the local school with other children from the huts and the older ones like me helped our mothers with the picking, first of fruit, then the hops, with the younger children joining in and helping during the school holidays. We experienced quite a lot of the war while we were in Kent over the next few years, what with the Spitfires shooting down the doodlebugs before they could get as far as London and the coastal air fights with the German Luftwaffe which we could watch overhead. However we were young and didn't understand war-time dangers.

Mrs L.I. Carter

Different Measures

It is important to make a distinction between measuring hops with a bushel basket from a bin (the method used in the Weald) and that of measuring with a six-bushel tally basket which was the practice in the Faversham area.

Dr Philip W. Bowden

110

Revisiting Old Haunts

In 1998 I took my caravan down to Painters farm caravan site and invited all my surviving aunts, cousins and family down for a walk around the farm and the site where the old hop gardens were. Many stories were recounted and we had a picture taken of us all standing where the huts used to be. It turned out to be a lovely day. I have gathered all the Parry family hop photos together in an album and have pictures dating back from 1934 onwards. Although most of them are of the family outside our hut some show us picking. When I'd done this I wrote to the farmer, Simon Elworthy, to see if he could tell me when my gran first went to Plumford. Unfortunately his records only went back to the 1950s but his mother did recall the Parry name. He did, however, send me the pages of his ledger for 1955 which certainly mention our name. They make really interesting reading as they also list the other families who picked with us.

Kevin Parry

End of an Era

I went hopping at the same farm until I was twenty-one. That was the last time I saw my friend Maureen Harper from the East End of London. Sad to say, the machines took over after that, and that was the end of our hop-picking at Goose Green Farm. We miss it very much; those by-gone days, all the fun and companionship and seeing seasonal friends each year. I miss all the things we did, like sitting round the fire in the evenings, telling stories and talking to friends. I went and visited Goose Green Farm when everything had gone. I sat there on the grass with my mum. It was empty, but I thought of all the lovely memories we shared and I would love to do it all again. I am sixty-six now and a granny myself, but what stories we can tell our children and grandchildren of those happy days.

Pat and George Cole

A Breath of Fresh Air

An East Ender's fashion of holiday spending must of sheer necessity be one in which work occupies the larger share, and although the denizens of Belgravia and Kensington might smile to have 'hopping' considered in the light of a holiday, yet the time of hop harvest is anticipated with the greatest jubilance by his less fortunate brothers and sisters of the slums – particularly by the younger portions of East End humanity. 'It gives 'em a breath o' real fresh air every year,' explained a mother to us eagerly as we stood in the hop-ground of a well-known Army friend and looked down upon a prettier picture than we had lately seen. The hot sun had poured down between the trailing vines through a long morning and one by one the merry children had wearied and dropped off from play. Two of them, mere babies, had curled themselves up in a little brown heap on a bundle of sun-dried stalks and leaves. Mother, coming to see after her bairns, had thrown them a shawl and erected a much-maimed umbrella over their sleepy heads. 'This one,' she pointed to a tiny fair-haired girl, 'is ill today. She can't pick or anything. It's the sun I think.' We wondered for a minute that a baby like that should be expected to do ought but trot around and play, but glancing at the nearest bin we saw a small maiden of about four

The Larkin menfolk coping with feeding the baby!

summers, gravely and diligently picking away at her mother's side, doing her fervent best to swell the family gain. She was kept to it by an occasional 'Now then, Polly!' when her energies threatened to flag. She had picked three bucketsful since breakfast and was 'almost ready for dinner now.' We judged it not at all unlikely. Dinnertime is nowhere a more picturesque sight than in a hopfield. Practically, it is the grouping of a hundred picnics under exceptional difficulties. Frequently enough the fire of lighted brushwood refuses to bear the weight of the little grimy tin kettle put upon it to boil and, in a dilemma such as this, one of our two companions – an energetic worker from the Wesleyan East End Mission –

rushed forward to proffer her services to a distressed housewife. Between them they held a long pole over the crackling flames, from which dangled a saucepan of ready-mixed tea, sugar and milk and to which they valiantly hung on until it simmered to their mutual satisfaction. Just beyond sat a group of dark-eyed gipsy children, brown as berries with their fresh-air existence and refreshingly hungry in comparison to their pale-faced brothers and sisters from slumdom.

Extract from the Salvation Army's monthly magazine The Deliverer, *October 1890, supplied by Kevin Parry*

A Big Job

The family of farmers I worked for had hops growing on three of their fields, which totalled 180 acres. Now you can understand hop-picking was a big job and although it was hard labour there was a lot of happiness in the gardens. I used to like it when the older ladies from London started singing all the old songs and everyone joined in. There was merriment and real neighbourly love all around. Only once did I have to settle a serious row between two families over a dispute regarding a row of hops and which of the two families should pick them.

Ted Bingham

The Old Tin Bath

I will always remember my mother bathing me in a tin bath the night before we were due to go down to Kent, getting me ready to go hop-picking in the morning, down in

Goose Green Farm in Hadlow. We would arrive at my granny and auntie's hut. Our cousins would light the lamps and get out a mattress cover and fill it with straw. We children were so excited. We travelled down by an old removal lorry. It was great, all of us singing all the way down from Bermondsey. I was four years old at the time.

Pat Cole

An Urgent Exodus

When the sweltering heat of early summer bit into the life of London town there began the annual urgent exodus of the well-to-do from the wilderness of brick and stone which is the Metropolis. But what of the most needy class of all? The men, women and children of the many-roomed, overpopulated tenement houses who gasp for air during the greater part of the year. They cannot afford a suite of rooms at the seaside or a cottage on the moor. There is one unfailing field in which change is found by tens of thousands of the city's poorest people. It is the Kentish hop fields. Steaming along the main roads leading to the Garden of England is an almost ceaseless procession of wheeled traffic. Push-bikes, motorbikes in their thousands; pony carts and horse-drawn carts, a few; an occasional donkey and shay; uncountable hosts of motorcars, charabancs, lorries and vans predominate, all loaded to the limit, some with stocks of provisions, liquid and solid, for the hoppers, but all with vocal sightseers, particularly on the outward journey. They are for the most part somnolent on the

Pat Cole aged eighteen, with Maureen Harper and another friend, September 1952.

Frank Larkin's family outside their hop hut at Chambers Farm, Maidstone.

return trip. One charabanc bears a banner: Hop-Pickers' Campaign. The passengers in this car are Salvationists. The Army, following its earliest instincts, has 'gone to the people'. From the first trainload they have gone, together with a contingent of Slum Officers, skilled in the handling of slum-dwellers' problems, weaknesses and what not. Loving and serving these people as they do, what should be more natural than they should accompany them when they go, under the kindly approval of the British Commissioner. On weekdays the Slum Officers devote themselves to caring for the children while the mothers strip the hop bines. During the day refreshments are taken out to the pickers. Meetings are held, first aid rendered to the injured and many services given without stint or hope of reward. A farmer brought along a sackful of apples to the Slum Officers who

offered their thanks, but the farmer waved them aside, saying 'I have saved far more than this by reason of your presence and influence. The hop-pickers' youngsters used simply to strip my apple trees bare for me!' The Army assembles by their charabanc in attack formation and sing their challenge 'Whosoever will may come!' The Hopping crowd passes from the hostelry with a certain studied indifference as if to say 'Why must they come down here?' Sheer joy in their work causes the Salvationists to clap their hands as they sing 'Yes, we'll gather by the river.' What a joy it is to the children to see the Army come. They sing together with the Army a 'Sunshine' song. The little sprites revel in it.

Extract from the Salvation Army's magazine
The Deliverer, *November 1926 contributed*
by Kevin Parry

Electricity

I think that the pickers who came down to the farm where we were working were lucky, because all the huts were kept in very good condition. They all had electricity put in them from the main supply and the company not only paid for its installation, but the pickers had the use of the electricity free while they were down there. In the olden days it was just a case of a wood fire outside the huts for boiling up the kettle as well as for all the cooking, and there were candles or oil lamps for the light at night, but with the electricity there was a real improvement, and now there are electric kettles, electric fires, an electric cooker and even television in some huts: a real home from home. One old lady said to me the other day that she thinks it is cheaper to come here than to go to the seaside.

Ted Bingham

Can't Wait to be Back

Mum used to send me home about four o'clock to start the fire and put all the pots on to cook which she had prepared the night before, so when she came home everything was nearly ready to serve up. We did it this way because it got dark about 4.30 p.m. This carried on year after year and believe me I saw many mums crying because they were about to go home and wouldn't be back again until the next September came around. But when it was time to come again the next year they would be back and doing exactly the same thing they had done the previous year.

C. Norman

Soldiers' Convoys

In the war years I can remember the convoys of soldiers in their lorries driving by our hop garden gate to the common, going off to war, and all the hopping people making them cups of tea. It was in the early hours of the morning. It was very sad because nobody knew if they would ever return. Our tin huts were painted black on the outside during the war so the enemy aircraft couldn't see them from the sky.

Pat and George Cole

Courting in the Hop Fields

We enjoyed our life in the hop gardens: scrumping the apples and other fruit from the orchards, rides around the farm on the back of the tractor trailer used to collect all the boxes of picked fruit, the open air, the friendships of all the Londoners; they were mostly women there, all pleased to be out of London with their children as it was thought to be safer in the countryside during the war. It was a happy time for us from early May until late September. Above all it was a healthy time for us and especially the children. After the war I went to work, dressmaking in Hackney Wick, so I stayed home with Dad during weekdays in September, but Mum, Joyce and Benny still went to Chambers Farm, picking, and Dad and I went down to help them at the weekends and managed to pick on Saturday mornings. Then I met my future husband and he started coming down with us as well, right up until all the hand picking was finished at Chambers Farm. My sister Joyce married a Kent man in 1952 and she used to go with her in-laws to a hop farm at

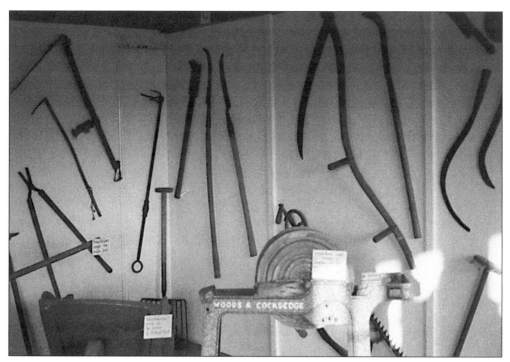

A display of old farming and hopping implements at the Hop Farm Country Park, Beltring.

Ulcombe. When her daughter Kim was born in 1957 she booked a bin on this farm for her and her mother. But this time Mum stayed in a house and slept in a bed. She thoroughly enjoyed picking the hops again but said it was much better living in the huts. Old habits die hard!

Mrs L.I. Carter

Wartime Tragedy

My sister died in 1997 and a month before then she rang me and said 'I wish we could go down hop-picking again,' although she would never go to Mr Mayes farm ever again. During the war in 1942 she left it late to go as her little girl was getting ready for school. But an unexploded bomb went off near the Elephant and Castle where she lived. My eldest sister was already down at Mayes Farm so my sister packed up and went down on the Friday. Sunday morning, her little girl was killed outright. Two young soldiers who were working for Mr Mayes went up home to my sister and told her what had happened. She was so distressed she cursed them both and they were upset and left, but she really didn't know what she was saying at the time. Before she died she said, 'I wish I could see those two young chaps again to tell them how sorry I am for the things I said to them.' During the war I had joined up in the WAAF and still always went down to one of my sisters when she was hop-picking. One year when I was about ten years old my mum left it later than usual to go down to the farm so Mr Mayes was full and we went to a farm in Paddock Wood by lorry. The farmer gave us a big barn to use. It had troughs all round the room and my mum made us cosy beds in them. It was great!

Ethel Chandler

A Harsh Life

We turned aside from the busy hum of healthy life to a shed which had been cleared for a picker's dwelling; a shed which had become a sacred place for the night, for the angel of death had stepped across its humble threshold. An old woman who had 'never been to the country afore, no, not never in her whole life,' poured out the story to us readily. She turned back the white sheet from the baby's still, sleeping face that we might look and pity. It wasn't in our heart to pity the bairn, released so early from and inevitable life of hardship and suffering, but to the mother, whose family were busy amongst the vines to earn sufficient bread 'to go round' that our sympathies did turn. We found her at last, picking busily beside her husband and little ones. Life had always gone so hardly, they told us, never a venture had they made, but it had somehow had an unfortunate ending. Even now they had not recovered themselves from the hardships of last winter. Yes, they had oftentimes been into the Salvation Army barracks in London and had heard what we were saying about the comfort and help that God could give, but they had never felt any of it. 'We thought too,' said the man, 'that it would have picked us up a bit to come down here and we felt cheerful over it, and undertook to pay the fare of that old woman to look after the very little children an' keep them straight, an' now there's the baby died –' He stopped abruptly and the mother's eyelashes winked hard to keep the tears back. Perhaps it was felt all the harder because in an egg box, fastened to the very next bin, there was perched the very bluest of all blue-eyed baby girls, and the little one, whose hands were folded across her breast yonder, was about the same age.

Extract from the Salvation Army's magazine
The Deliverer, October 1890, contributed by
Kevin Parry

Travellers

At Goose Green Farm we would see all the travellers and Romany folk. Lovely people, they were. There names were the Stone family from Southend, the Lawrence family from Middlesex and the Smiths from near Brighton. I was friends with Jean and Dereck Stone; their sister, Eileen Stone, pierced our ears having first greased them with margarine. I was fourteen at the time. My cousins, Pat and Sheila, had their ears pierced on the same day. There were Jimmy and Van Lawrence, Charles Smith, their mum and dad. We were very fond of all the travellers. They were great fun.

Pat Cole

Hit by a Land Mine

When we got down to Whitbreads Hop Farm Gran, Nance and Stella gave Mrs Fermor their ration books, as was normal if you went to stay with anyone then, then they went back to Tent Common to collect their suitcases and bags. The soldiers were coming onto the common and they soon got talking to the girls. They offered to give them a lift back to Tonbridge when they had finished their duties for the day. So Stella and Nance sat in the cookhouse with a number of the others and chatted. Planes started to come over again and it was said that one of them dropped an oil drum; but thinking about it now, it must have been a land mine. Everyone was blown up, Stella was killed and a number of others, including Nance, were severely injured. At the time, Nance didn't know that Stella had been killed, but one day a priest came round and asked if she wanted anything. Nance said she wanted to know where Stella was and the priest went away to find out. When he came back he said that Stella had gone. Nance said 'Where? Back to London without me?' and then she looked up she saw my Aunt May coming up the ward crying so she knew then what had happened. Mrs Fermor had heard about the bomb and when the girls didn't return she went to the hospital to find them. She saw Nance was badly hurt and went to visit her regularly. Mrs Fermor had a son who was a soldier and he visited Nance too for all the six months she was in hospital. She had a piece of shrapnel in her shoulder. It was about a foot long. Nance and Alf became very fond of each other and they eventually married and lived in Tonbridge for the rest of their lives. Nance died in 1997 and was buried in Paddock Wood Cemetery, ironically next to five German airmen killed in the same raid.

Louisa Barrington

After the War

At the end of the war I got married and we had a one-bedroomed flat in Swan Lane, over the top of the Bygraves family. Max Bygraves' mum was ever so kind when I had my two girls. I broke away from my own family for the picking and found a nice place at Seal near Sevenoaks to go picking. When I was expecting my third I moved to Mottingham, SE9. When she was born she had a cleft palate and wasn't very strong and ended up at the Great Ormond Street Hospital in London. My mum said to take her hop-picking, as it would do her good. The farmer was great and let my friend and I go down to our hut two weeks early so we went cob-nut picking. He even let me have my own toilet with a padlock. How I miss it all! Why did they stop it? I have a photo of my dad pea-picking with two of my brothers (Tom and Joe Ash) at Mr Betts' farm in West Malling. I think my mum knew every farm in the area because when Mayes had finished she would cart us all off to another one to help out. She never wanted to come home!

Ethel Chandler

Still Go Down to Marden

Although we're in our sixties now we still very often talk about hopping and still go down to Marden. We walk over the land where the huts used to be and try to work out whereabouts our hut was, but everything seems so much smaller now. My brothers still go down about twice a year.

Joan Lewer

Pat Cole with the rest of her family at Goose Green, September 1949.

Wretched Huts

'Wretched huts, unfit for the proper housing of pigs,' wrote a London newspaper last week in description of the usual arrangements made for the accommodation of city hoppers. On some farms we know this to be true, on others it is decidedly not the case, the lodges provided being quite up to the standard of the people who temporarily inhabit them – healthier dwellings (despite all drawbacks) than the close, dark, foetid rooms in which they sicken during the rest of the year. Coming as it does in the slackest time of the year for London work, the hop holiday, with its long, healthful days of out-door labour, light enough for the weakest, its plentiful mede of sweet, fresh air and invigorating tonic aroma is welcomed by all the city poor who can avail themselves of it, and well it is for those who are able. Yet there is another side to the whole question. Where

the hoppers' huts are rain-tight and draught-proof, the space is frequently so limited that men, women and children are much more often herded together than 'accommodated'. Much evil comes of it – drinking is freely indulged; foul language abounds; quarrelling rages; in the spoiling of tempers consequent upon great inconvenience and overcrowding the children suffer, often painfully. Indecent habits are common and open and many a hitherto pure girl goes back to the city contaminated, to drift untimely in the streets. 'Then it is better to abolish hop-picking altogether!' exclaims some reader, horror-stricken. Not at all, good friend. Do it on model lines. It was to see it done that way that we journeyed to Biggenden Farm, Paddock Wood. We were instructed that we would find there a mixture of Shelter women, Slum soldiers and many whose only acquaintance with the Salvation Army had been on the fringes of open-air

Sunday morning services were held for the adults at the hop gardens, and children could attend their own Sunday school (courtesy of the Hop Farm Country Park).

Whitechapel meetings. About fifty of these women had set off a week earlier from Cannon Street under the guardianship of Captain Richardson of the Rescue Training Garrison. Hoppers' luggage, not always of the picturesque, pots, pans, rags, bedding, broken crockery, is bundled together perfectly regardless of appearances. It was with a good deal of interest we set off to see the working of this model plan, but what a day for hopping, to be sure! Rain, steady and pitiless, drenched the London streets as we ran for the train. 'You are never going in

this?' we asked of a girl. 'Why, yes I am,' she replied.

Extract from the Salvation Army's magazine The Deliverer, *October 1892, contributed by Kevin Parry*

The usefulness for raising extra cash, the companionship and the romance of the hopfields were recognized by many authors, including Charles Dickens, George Orwell and Daniel Defoe, who mentioned Kent hops in their stories.

Defoe called Kent Weald 'the Mother of Hop grounds, being the first place in England where hops were planted in any quantity.' (Tour through England and Wales)

Referring to Whitbreads Hop Farm, Siegfried Sassoon wrote in his Memoirs of a Fox-Hunting Man: 'It was unusual to find more than two kilns on a farm, but there was one had twenty and its company of white cowls was clearly visible from our house on the hill.'

'Say for what were hop-yards meant,
Or why was Burton built on Trent?
Oh many a peer of England brews –
Livelier liquor than the Muse,
And malt does more than Milton can –
To justify God's way to man.'

Mr Jingle, a friend of Dickens' Mr Pickwick, exclaimed: 'Kent, sir? Everybody knows Kent! Apples, cherries, hops and women!'

Hop-Picking Changes

I cannot exactly remember the year hop-picking, as we knew it, began to change. But apparently students were brought in to pick hops because they were cheaper than employing traditional pickers. Then of course the machines took over doing the job and hundreds of people lost their way of life for ever. My late father used to say 'Two steps forward and one step back is the price we pay for progress.' I am sure he was right. Almost fifty years have passed since my childhood experience of hop-picking days; those happy, carefree times still live on in my memory. Sadly, those days are lost, but for me – and, I'm sure, for many of London's 'hop-picking kids' – it was such a magical time of life.

Maureen E. White

The Hop Garden

Wooden soldiers cross the field
Wired and strung to bear the yield.
We crown each hill with spindly twirls
Of hops trained by these comely girls,
And when they reach six inches high
Round the strings then gently tie.
Dig them well and dress with mould
And you will grow a crop worth gold.
Then, as the bines reach to the sun,
Continue twiddling till growth's done.
As autumn comes each bine will flower
Bearing forth its Goldings shower.
September, down the serried aisles
The pickers work with cheerful smiles
To earn their boots and Christmas fare,
Happy in the country air.

HH

Hard Work

We look back and think of our lovely holidays, but in reality it was hard work and if it rained, well it was terrible and of course every morning there was always a very heavy dew which soaked us as we picked.

Kevin Parry

An Uncomplicated Life

The generation of children that have been through those tough war years appreciate the uncomplicated way of life in the hop fields of the fifties and I do believe them to be the best years any generation will know. Our last hop-picking trip was in 1955. Not too long after that they brought in the machines to do the job. Because we were not wanted as pickers any more, people in the East End had to start taking other kinds of holidays and those wonderful hop-picking days were gone for ever.

Rita Game

A Typical Farmer

I cannot remember how long our hopping season lasted; however, during the time we were there my cousins and I had a great time. Scrumping in the orchards and chasing cattle always got us a good ticking off by the farmer when we got caught. Although at times hop-picking was tiring it did have its rewards: country life, fresh air and the social side, together with a few extra coppers in the family purse. The farmer was good, too, and a typical farmer he was: dressed in tweeds with matching tweed hat with brim pulled down, he wore leather gaiters and boots and carried a stout walking stick. He made regular visits to the hoppers to socialize and make sure of their well-being.

Clive Gwyer

Crushed Hops

On the last day of picking it was traditional to throw someone in the bin on top of the hops, but a lot of the parents didn't like it because it crushed the hops and made the measure small for when the next tally was taken.

Maureen Vinall (née Jenkins)

Hopping Marriage

My mother, Doris Turner (née French) was a regular picker in Kent. She met my father during the six weeks of hop picking holidays at Goudhurst which lasted from August to late September.

Philip Turner

Country Friends

I still pay weekend visits to the old places during the summer. I often meet up with the country friends I made during past hop-picking seasons when I went down with my parents. My family and I have been to weddings, funerals and engagement parties of these country folk who have been our true friends and I feel that I'm one of them. They visit me in my London home when they come up here and I visit them by invitation. I say this because if country folk don't accept you, forget it, because even if you won the lottery they couldn't care less – they only accept you as a friend if they take to you and I'm happy that they accepted me. I hope there is a hop garden in Heaven.

C. Norman

Old Songs

Aunt Bob used to sing all the popular songs and sometimes she'd change the words with a few rude ones thrown in. One I remember was:

My old man's a dustman,
He wears a dustman's hat.

Coopers at work making barrels (courtesy of the Hop Farm Country Park).

He killed five thousand Germans
Now what do you think of that?
One lay here, one lay there,
One lay round the corner,
One poor soul with a bullet up 'is 'ole
Was crying out for water.
Water, water came at last.
'I don't want your water!
Just give it to your daughter.
Ask Old Brown to tea
With all his family,
If he don't come
We'll tickle his bum
With a stick of celery.'

Bob Orris

About the Hop Plant

The hop (*Humulus lupulus*) is a popular and hardy Kentish plant useful for covering fences, sheds, arches, pergolas and to decorate the house. The foliage lasts from spring to autumn and dies back each winter. The bine grows up to 20ft each year and needs to be planted in the sun or semi-shade in well-drained soil, supported on strong coconut-fibre twine. To protect from mildew etc., spray regularly with fungicide such as Nimrod. Female flowers become clusters of hops in autumn and are excellent for drying arrangements. Hops are cultivated for their fruit which gives the characteristic bitter flavour to beer.

The Hop Farm Country Park

Bomb Craters

One day during the war we had sixty-two bombs dropped on our farm! There was one crater which was so big it could have taken three or four double-decker buses. You see when the bombers didn't get to London they turned and they used to drop their bombs on Kent so they didn't have to travel back to Germany with them. Once, I had all my windows blown out. We still carried on with the work in the hop fields but it wasn't safe, really. When you heard the air-raid siren you all ducked down where you were. My boy was a toddler then and he was a terror for undressing himself. We'd be picking and the raid would come. The other pickers would say 'It's all right, Alice, I'm picking up his shoes,' 'I've got his vest' and I'd just see this little naked body coming along and I had to run and get him because the pilots in the German planes would machine-gun you. If the baby was in the pram and there was a raid you ran with the pram and tipped it over in the ditch by the hop field, so it shielded the baby and they didn't see you. My husband, he'd be ploughing and my boys used to call out 'Dad! Dad! There's a doodlebug coming!' They knew because they'd make a whistling noise and you'd see it go by. The boys used to get frightened in case it came near him, you see. You'd just see this big flame and once that flame went out, then it'd land and explode. They flew ever so low. You could see them coming at you over the hop poles. And the V2s were the worst because you never saw them. They just came and you were gone. In our house

we had what you called a table shelter and we all slept underneath that. It's like a big iron table with a bottom; a Morrison shelter. But you could have an Anderson shelter in the garden instead if you wanted to.

Alice Heskitt

Salvation Army Work

Hop fields of all sizes and peopled with all kinds of pickers stretch around us throughout Kent. Some employ six or seven hundred pickers for several weeks at a time. For the most part the people who live in the neighbourhood arrange to work in the same field – friends and parties and Salvation soldiers getting together as far as possible. Thus in one garden of thirty people we found twenty-six of the thirty saved either by the Salvationists, Church Army soldiers or the Railway Mission. In some places our soldiers turn out in such force that they marched to and from the hop fields singing Army hymns. The captain at Canterbury finds herself compelled to do her visiting in the hop fields since nobody is at home. At East Peckham so many people work late in distant gardens that the officer has closed her barracks except on Sundays, and works every night in a tent. The sanitary and moral conditions of the hopping houses have doubtless been much improved of later years, but the long, low, crowded shed-like buildings and the little dark tents floored with straw and the blasphemous babble of the yards where the women and children herd after sunset are hardly even yet what you would like to put your son or daughter into. Some [officers] offend the prejudices of Londoners by putting on airs. One invited hop-pickers to his meetings but was told they were not hop-pickers but were down for their health. Our headquarters are two little cottages, each with a garden, in Tunbridge. Each cottage has two rooms below, three above. The lower front room is styled the Staff Room by the girls. In it work three staff officers. The round table is the Office of All the World. A cupboard in one corner is our Trade Headquarters. The walls are covered with maps of Disposition of Forces and are brightened by a text or two and an Army flag. We hold long regular, open-air meetings in the Public Hall all day Sunday and spend as much time as possible in the Hop Gardens spreading salvation. One Salvation Army officer owns a hop garden which is eminently respectable. Our quiet walk home after our second Sunday meeting ended in a frantic rush to save a terrified little black baby. Its mother had tucked it under one arm while she defended herself from her husband who had dragged her from the lodging house onto the main street and was hitting her. 'Wait till the Charlton boys come back from hopping and they'll make an end of you,' one Dover lad said to us. Meantime we are praying that our brigade may fall in with the Charlton boys and make Salvationists of them. We walked across to Paddock Wood to Mr Welfear's hop garden. Scores and hundreds of pickers date their conversion from the season they spent here.

Extract from the Salvation Army's magazine The Deliverer, *October 1892, contributed by* *Kevin Parry*

Italian POWs

The Italian prisoners of war used to come on our farm helping to do odd jobs. My kids loved them. They used to get a rabbit and kill it and then they'd cook it over a fire and my boys would be down there enjoying themselves with them.

Alice Heskitt

My Favourite Days

Sundays were my favourite days of hop-picking. Everyone relaxed after a long week in the hop fields. We children virtually had the whole day to ourselves, thereby giving the adults a well-earned break from us. We spent the time climbing trees, playing hide-and-seek and various other games. Later in the afternoon we would gather hazelnuts, pick wild damsons and blackberries, scrump apples from the orchards then make for the haystack and, gaining footholds, gradually haul ourselves to the top. Once there, we edged the bales outwards a little with our feet before wiggling down into the warm hay. Perched up there we feasted on our spoils while planning what adventures we would have next.

Maureen E. White

Pot Boiling

There was a lady who went hopping at the same place as us each year at Smalls Farm, Cowden, near Penshurst. She was named Mrs Saunders who, for a number of years, set herself up in the corner of the hut field with a surround of sacking attached to sticks and she had her fire in the middle, always with a pot boiling. Her eyes always appeared to be watering from the constant smoke but she loved it. I could go on all day about the six weeks in Kent: I might forget what happened yesterday but never what happened in those good old days.

Mrs Q. Moody

The Hurricane

In 1987 there was a violent storm across south-east England and particularly in the Tonbridge area. Quite a lot of hop farms in the area were badly damaged and it was lucky that their hop crops were already in. Whitbread's Beltring hop farm lost 180,000 tiles off their oast 'bells' as well as other structural damage. It cost £400,000 just to replace the tiles. Local trains and buses weren't able to run to time and it was hard to get to work. The builders in the area had a field day; they had more work than they could handle. A lot of pubs were damaged too and, as many roofs had been ripped off with the high winds, everyone wanted their work done at once. There was a roaring trade in candles when the power went down.

Once, the whole of Whitbread's 1,000-acre farm was under hops but by 1989 hops covered only 110 acres and 650 acres was arable. Some of the farm's older workers, turned pensioners, lived in thirty-four brick cottages on the estate and continued to live there despite the farm being opened to the public in 1982. Portable buildings had to be brought in to keep the place running but the farm still had 95,000 visitors there that year. At least the beautiful Shire horses were saved and they got a new stable block when the corrugated iron sheets were ripped from the roof of the old block.

George Green

The Garden of England

Well if they got rid of the machines and brought back the bins I would be there – and I know hundreds and hundreds of old hoppers who would join me – picking hops and singing in the Garden of England.

Rose Elliot Amis

Where Can I Still Pick Hops?

While these former ways of life are sadly missed, it is still possible for ex-hoppers to enjoy something of the old life and traditions. When giving talks on hop-picking I am frequently asked to recommend where hops are to be seen and where visitors would be welcome for a day's outing. Fortunately there are still a number of farms where hops are grown, the old traditions kept up and where hopeful hoppers can collect their lucky bine, and I include here a list of places where you would be welcome to visit. Sadly, many hop farms are closing down – even as I write I was given news of yet another which has finished in the Faversham area.

The Hop Farm Country Park, Beltring, Paddock Wood, was formerly Whitbreads' and the largest hop garden in Kent. It is now owned by the Pollard family who still grow hops the traditional way, offering ex-hoppers a warm welcome and the opportunity to pick their own bine in early September. Here you can see the largest array of oast houses in Kent and there is an excellent exhibition on hop-picking, complete with sound effects, a display of tools, rides in brewery drays pulled by the famous Whitbread Shire horses, a restaurant and a shop selling hop products, books about hop-picking and you can even buy your own hop plant to take home to grow in your garden. Hoppers are welcome to take their caravan or tent and stay on the farm for the weekend, picking hops by hand during the September season. The 'Happy Hoppers' Room' (named by Mrs R. Vaughan, one of the contributors to *Voices of Kent Hop-Pickers*) caters for the needs of toddlers and children of all ages will enjoy visiting the small animals farm and the craft sections. (Telephone: 01622-872068. Fax: 01622-872630)

Shepherd Neame Master Brewers is situated in Court Street in the ancient town of Faversham, ME13 7AX. An interesting tour can be made of this 300-year-old brewery and tours are run by Shepherd Neame on a regular basis, but it is wise to book well in advance as there is often a waiting list for both groups and individual visitors. (Telephone: 01795-532206. Fax: 01795-538907)

Faversham town on the A2 holds a lively and well established annual hop festival over the first weekend in September. It is run by the Sheerness District Office Community Services. Among the many attractions are Morris dancers, country dancing, hop bines for sale, stilt walkers, a Hoppers' Ball on the Saturday evening, country music, a warm welcome in all the pubs, and accommodation and good food at The Swan and Harlequin (near Shepherd Neame's brewery), should you wish to stay the night. The streets are lined with a multitude of stalls selling everything from freshly made cakes and preserves, hand-made goods, second-hand books, crafts and antiques to hop bines, home-made cider, healthful fruit and vegetables fresh from local farms. (Telephone: 01795-580068. Fax: 01795-669097)

The Fleur de Lis Heritage Centre run by the Faversham Society in Preston Street, Faversham, has a gold nugget of a museum (newly extended in 2000) with displays about hop-picking and cultivation as well as other aspects of local history, also a wide selection of books about the area, many of which the Society publishes itself. The museum, which is run entirely by volunteers, opens all through the year and has a good display of hop-picking-related exhibits. Of interest to ex-hoppers are traditional horse brasses showing hop-pickers, china thimbles depicting hop-picking in Faversham in 1897 and the oast houses at Macknade Farm, picture postcards of hopping as well as hop-picking books, including *The Truth about Hop Picking in Faversham*, *Hopping in Verse*, *The Annual Hop: London to Kent* and *Voices of Kent Hop Pickers*. The Centre will send their publications list on request and items can be bought by post. It is well worth a visit. Museum Curator is John Culmer and the shop manager, Peter Faulkner. (telephone: 01795-534542. E-mail: faversham@btinternet.com)

The Kent Museum for Rural Life at Cobtree grows hops traditionally and also holds a festival in September when they pull the bines in their own hop field. Stalls display a variety of country crafts. The old farmhouse offers traditional hoppers' meals and there is a variety of farm animals and a collection of horse-drawn farm vehicles. In the well-preserved oast house is an interesting display of how hops are harvested, dried and pocketed. A 'Darling Buds of May' exhibition was set up in 1997. (Telephone: 01622-763936. Fax: 01622-662024)

'Essentially Hops' is the Barker family business at Parsonage Farm, School Lane, Bekesbourne, Canterbury, CT4 5ER (off the A2). This active hop farm supplies lucky bines in season (September to December) as well as hop plants to grow in your garden. Visitors are welcome to look round. The farm specializes in attractive hop garlands, bunches of dried hops, grasses, dried flowers either by the bunch or in kit form, as well as pots, baskets and containers. Individual tuition is offered on making hop garlands and flower arrangements. The farm's website is worth checking. (Telephone: 01227-830666. E-mail: info@essentiallyhops.co.uk. Web: www.essentiallyhops.co.uk)

Lamberhurst, a small, attractive village off the A21, holds a smaller festival at the beginning of September. Forstall Farm in Lamberhurst has hop bines for sale during the season.

If you would like to do your hop-picking abroad for a change, take a trip to **Poperinge, Holland**: a historic town surrounded by active hopfields and boasting the national Hop Museum.

A converted oast house near Paddock Wood.